FASCINATE

C. 2

FASCINATE

Your 7 Triggers to
Persuasion and Captivation

SALLY HOGSHEAD

HARPER
BUSINESS

An Imprint of HarperCollins*Publishers*
www.harpercollins.com

To Quinton and Azalea,

my fascinations

HarperCollins books may be purchased for educational, business, or sales promotional use. For information, please write: Special Markets Department, HarperCollins Publishers, 10 East 53rd Street, New York, NY 10022.

Designed by Renato Stanisic

Library of Congress Cataloging-in-Publication Data

Hogshead, Sally.
Fascinate : your 7 triggers to persuasion and captivation / Sally Hogshead.
p. cm.
Includes index.
ISBN 978-0-06-171470-2
1. Marketing—Psychological aspects. 2. Advertising—Psychological aspects. I. Title.
HF5415.34.H65   2010
658.8001'9—dc22   2009038607

11 12 13 14 ov/rrd 10 9

Contents

The amnesiac and the maze • Papyrus print ads • Trends driving distraction • Rise of the ADD world • Goldfish and nine seconds • Paying attention vs. earning attention • Shutting out messages • The Fascination Economy

Some ideas take off, but most fizzle • Esperanto death sentence • Gold Hallmarks of a fascinating message • Provoking reactions • Creating advocates • Cultural shorthand • Inciting conversation • Forcing competitors to realign • Social revolutions • Hype • Naming your baby with Google • A man named David Scott

The Most Fascinating Person in the Room • The F Score • High-Scoring Personalities • More Fascinating Isn't Always Better • Fascination versus Likability or Respect • Famous High-Scorers • Ultra-Scoring Personalities • Low-Scoring Personalities • Not Fascinating Yet? Don't Panic, You're on the Road

PART II: THE SEVEN FASCINATION TRIGGERS

Meet Your New Arsenal: Lust, Mystique, Alarm, Prestige, Power, Vice, and Trust

Marilyn Monroe's wet voice • Craving • "But I *want* it!" • Increasing desire for boring brands • Stop thinking, start feeling • Testosterone-drenched saliva • Body odor

alpha stance • Celebrity monkey paparazzi • Controlling the environment • The most fascinating organization in the world? • Reward and punishment • Potent, or impotent

PART III: THE FASCINATION PLAN OF ATTACK
How to Make Your Own Messages More Fascinating

Ideas kept under lock and key • Three stages • Workshop program overview

Preface

Witchcraft, Green Peas, and Sigmund Freud

More weight!" cried the old man, begging to be crushed more quickly. "More weight!"

It was the summer of 1692, in Salem village. The old man's ribs snapped one by one, in sickening succession, each audible to the hundreds of townsfolk encircling his execution. But his pleas were answered instead with the same slow addition of stones upon his chest. For two days, six large men lifted stone and rock onto Giles Corey's torso. But Corey refused to confess to any charges, asking only for more weight to speed his death. The sheriff stood over him, impatiently waiting for a confession, using his cane to push the old man's tongue back inside his mouth. At last, Corey was silenced by the final stone dropping upon his breast. His crime?* Giles had been accused of "fascination," casting a spell that left his victims powerless

---

* Good news: Massachusetts no longer issues death sentences on charges of fascination.

to resist. The grand jury decreed he had enchanted the townspeople, mesmerizing them so fully that they became immobilized with captivation. Under the spell of fascination, they became hostage to his thoughts, losing the ability to think rationally or protest.* The concept of fascination didn't begin with Giles Corey's execution in Salem village. Throughout cultures, across the continents, since the birth of civilization itself, people have studied the ways in which fascination influences behavior. The word "fascination" comes from the ancient Latin, *fascinare*, "to bewitch."

All around the world, ancient cultures were fascinated with fascination. The Romans believed it was an evil curse, and for protection worshipped one of the earliest Latin divinities: Fascinus, the god of fascination.† In Mesopotamia, Persians believed fascination could cause deadly maladies. In Constantinople, citizens painted passages from the Koran upon their houses to defend their families from the spell of fascination's evil eye. Fortunately, by 280 B.C., Greece's first pastoral poet, Theocritus, seemed to have found a safeguard: an old woman's spit. During the Renaissance, the bookshelves of Europe were filled with weighty tomes on the subject. *De Fascino* defined fascination as "an open covenant with Satan . . . witchcraft of the eyes, or words . . . to so compel men that they are no longer free, nor of sane understanding." A hundred years later, *Tractatus de Fascinatione* warned against lounging in bed too late in the morning wearing nightcaps

---

* Giles Corey is a character in Arthur Miller's 1953 play about the Salem witch trials, *The Crucible*. Of slightly less cultural significance is that Giles Corey also inspired a song titled "More Weight," by a band named iLiKETRAiNS.

† Fascinus was worshipped by "vestal virgins" (young girls selected to remain virgins for thirty years or else be buried alive), and Roman children wore phallic-shaped amulet necklaces to symbolize him.

(yes, nightcaps), or breaking a religious fast on green peas (yes, green peas).

How to prevent and cure? In many cases, the remedy seems almost worse than the disease: the skin of a hyena's forehead, dust in which a mule had rolled, and a broth stewed from the ashes of a hangman's rope. Not exactly goods you could pick up on an afternoon Costco run. In the absence of hyena forehead skin, it seems one could also lick the skin of a child's forehead.

If all that sounds like quackery, let's consult a doctor with whom you might be more familiar: Sigmund Freud. In 1921, Freud labeled the relationship between a therapist and a patient as "fascination," a form of hypnosis. He went on to describe romantic love as a state in which an individual becomes so submissively engrossed in his object of "fascination" that he becomes hypnotized, losing his critical faculties, in "bondage of love."* Freud, apparently, wasn't the only one comparing fascination with hypnosis. The 1911 edition of the *Encyclopaedia Britannica* describes fascination as a "hypnotic condition, marked by muscular contraction, but with consciousness and power of remembrance."

Even our modern *Webster's Dictionary* sounds a bit sinister in comparing fascination to witchcraft: "bewitching, or enchanting . . . the exercise of a powerful or irresistible influence on the affections or passions; unseen, inexplicable influence."

Yet as we'll see, the ability to fascinate isn't witchcraft or hypnotism. And it doesn't come from wearing nightcaps or eating green peas. It is a tool. Rather than something to be

---

* Speaking of Freud and phallic symbols: *Fascinare* is Latin for "fascinate." *Fascinum* is Latin for "erect penis." Draw your own conclusions.

feared, it is a discipline to be mastered. Fascination is born of a natural instinct to influence the behavior of others. But the key to mastering fascination is effectively activating the seven triggers:

LUST creates craving for sensory pleasure.
MYSTIQUE lures with unanswered questions.
ALARM threatens with negative consequences.
PRESTIGE earns respect through symbols of achievement.
POWER commands and controls.
VICE tempts with "forbidden fruit," causing us to rebel
   against norms.
TRUST comforts us with certainty and reliability.

Whether you realize it or not—whether you intend to or not—you're already using the seven triggers. The question is, are you using the *right* triggers, in the *right* way, to get your desired result? By mastering the triggers, your ideas become more memorable, your conversations more persuasive, and your relationships more lasting.

Across the ages, scholars have described the powers of fascination. Century after century, they've told us how to recognize when someone is in a state of fascination. Society after society, they've defined why fascination matters. They've described repeatedly, and at length, the ways in which fascination affects decision making. Yet throughout two thousand years of writings, one question remains unanswered. And this is the most important question of all:

How can *you* become more fascinating?

Let's find out.

Introduction

What Is "Fascination," Exactly?

How I Became Fascinated with Fascination

Growing up in my family, earning attention wasn't a recreational pursuit. It was a matter of survival. Like any youngest child, I had to compete with older siblings for attention. By toddlerhood I'd honed numerous strategies, from the strategically executed tantrum to the art of asking, "Why? Why? Why?"

But then, when I turned seven, I was forced to raise my game. That year, my sister was number one in the world in her swimming event (and went on to win three gold medals in the Olympics), and my brother was accepted into Harvard. The height of my achievement up to that point? Gold stars for finger painting.* It was then that I learned my first lesson in fascination: A competitive environment demands a more captivating message. Perhaps it won't come as a surprise that I went

---

* Yes, I've since worked out my issues on the shrink's couch, thanks for asking. (As if having the last name "Hogshead" weren't bad enough.)

into marketing. Now I create messages for companies whose competitive environments demand captivating messages.

In a distracted and overwhelmed world, everything— including you, your communication, and your relationships— fights tooth and nail to get noticed. Without fascination we can't sell products off shelves, persuade shareholders to invest, teach students to read, or convince spouses to vacation in Bora Bora next February. Yet with fascination on your side, not only can you vacation in Bora Bora; you can also unlock your own creative potential.

The Boy and the Chandeliers

Watching the boy, you might assume he was either daydreaming or bored. But actually the opposite was true. He was coming alive. Pulse accelerating, pupils dilating, sweat prickling, he stared at the iron chandeliers overhead. Suspended by chains from the ceiling, these chandeliers swung in graceful arcs after their wax candles were lit. The boy watched, hypnotized. He realized something: The chandeliers took an equal number of heartbeats to complete each arc, every single time, whether that arc was big or small. This boy wasn't merely "interested" in the swaying chandeliers. He wasn't "paying attention" to them. He was *fascinated* by them, and their movement. They swung back and forth. Back and forth. Like a pendulum.

It was during this moment of fascination in the Pisa Cathedral that a seventeen-year-old Galileo unlocked the most basic rhythm in the universe: *isochronism*, the quantum leap in physics that soon led to his invention of the pendulum clock, which led to modern timekeeping.

Even if you haven't invented timekeeping, you've experienced this spellbinding focus. It's when you become lost in a moment, losing track of time and the world around, completely focused on a person or message. When you fascinate other people, not only do they focus on you and your message but they're also more likely to believe, care about, and retell your message.

Yet until now, the act of fascinating others has been an unpredictable occurrence, a product of luck or timing or mysticism, rather than an ability to be directed at will. But now, using both art *and* science, we'll clear the mystery. Along the way we'll uncover *what* fascinates people, and *why* it fascinates them. We'll hear from leading experts in psychology, evolutionary biology, neurology, and other -ologies, all shaken and served with a slice of pop culture.* To understand why we become fascinated, and how we fascinate others, we'll delve into results from the first in-depth national marketing survey on fascination. Developed and executed specifically for this book, the Kelton Study includes more than a thousand people around the country in a broad range of ages, industries, and professional levels. The Kelton Study found that people want to be *fascinated*, and they want to be *fascinating*. Two branding implications:

- People would be willing to pay almost a week's salary to be the most fascinating person in any situation. (A big opportunity if your brand can help consumers feel more *fascinating* in their own lives.)

- People want to feel fascinated by a product or experience, and will pay more—often far more—for a brand that

---

* We'll point to marketing, but this book isn't just for marketers. Marketing is just a metaphor for the modern world, because every day, in every relationship, we're "marketing" our ideas to be heard.

fascinates them. (A big opportunity if your brand can help consumers feel more *fascinated*.)

Companies will add more value, and compete more effectively, by activating one or more of the seven triggers. Those who don't will be pushed aside or, worse, forgotten. Messages that fail to fascinate will become irrelevant. It's that simple. This might not be fair. But as Salem villager Giles Corey can attest, fascination doesn't always play nice.

We all have certain behaviors that don't exactly make sense, even to ourselves. We make certain choices, and take certain actions, without understanding exactly *why*. Here's why: In a state of fascination, we don't think and act quite logically. We do things we don't understand, we believe messages we don't agree with, and we buy things we don't even want. At its most extreme, fascination short-circuits the logical evaluation process.

Rather than coolly analyzing a decision, we're gripped by deeply rooted triggers. We might think we're in control of our own choices, but much of the time, we're not. The seven triggers are. Triggers explain why people join suicidal cults, or develop bizarre fetishes, or willingly obey tyrannical dictators. More commonly (but just as irrationally), they buy sports cars they can't afford, procrastinate on major deadlines, or fall in love with the "wrong" person. Yet once you understand the triggers behind them, these decisions begin to make sense. A sneak preview of some examples we'll explore:

When does a billion-dollar anti-drug program actually make kids *more* likely to do drugs?

The U.S. government spends $1.13 billion annually on an anti-drug program named DARE. Not only does DARE not keep kids off drugs, it makes them *more* likely to use drugs. This massive program increases drug use because it unintentionally fascinates kids, using the vice trigger. It's not just teenagers who respond to vice: This trigger tempts us all to occasionally rebel and experiment.

Why did millions of people trust Hitler?

Hitler activated the trust trigger with horrible effectiveness. How? Trust relies on consistency. Hitler knew this. He exploited a fundamental truth about trust: If you tell a lie big enough, and keep repeating it, and deny any contradicting input, eventually people will come to believe it. No matter how illogical or poorly crafted the argument may be, followers are almost forced to trust the message, because it's all they know. To understand the lessons behind Hitler's tyranny, and to see which brands use the same principles, turn to the trust trigger. And a few pages later, you'll also find out why childhood obesity can be overcome with principles similar to Hitler's.

When is a flower worth more than the house it's planted in front of?

In the late seventeenth century, the world experienced what many economists believe was the first economic bubble. This bubble wasn't in housing, or currency, or credit; it was in tulips. Much like the real estate bubble of 2006, it all started with rumors of outrageous profits. The price of tulips grew higher, and tulips became a symbol of status—a botanical Louis Vuitton bag. The prestige trigger began to obsess both the status-conscious and investors. Prices soared to such extraordinary heights that an entire network of values flipped on its head, and the price of a single bulb began to exceed the average person's salary. Yes, it seems cuckoo in retrospect. But we all make decisions based on the prestige trigger, seeking respect and validation from our peers.

Why, exactly, do humans smile?
When other animals pull their lips back from their teeth, it usually means they're about to attack. Why, then, is smiling a sign of appeasement among humans? Finally, after many years of debate, anthropologists solved the riddle. As you'll see in Part I, it has nothing to do with how it makes your face *look*, and everything to do with how it makes your voice *sound*. It's one of the many ways in which you're already using fascination cues (and always have).

And finally, there's perhaps the most important question of all:

Which of the seven triggers should you be applying to your own work and life?
To answer this question, allow me to direct you to the chapter on mystique. Here, we'll explore the greatest puzzles of the world: from unsolved murders, to secret formulas, to conspiracy theories. Under the spell of mystique, people willingly do things they'll regret, follow trends they dislike, and even buy products they despise. You'll find out why you're more motivated by curiosity than by answers, and how you can use suspense to your advantage when communicating with others. You'll discover that the most surefire way to kill mystique is . . . *to give away the answer.*

To answer this last question above, I'm going to trigger a little mystique myself, and won't give away all the answers quite yet. Read on.

In the meantime, I will reveal this: Many of our choices are, in fact, not choices at all. Our best friends and favorite foods, our pets and pet peeves, all are contingent upon the seven triggers. The movies we see, the cereal we buy, we often don't *choose* to be fascinated by these things any more than we *choose* to feel thirsty or fall asleep. It's the same with the opinions we believe, the jokes that make us laugh, and the person with whom we fall in (and out of) love. We're in control far less than we fancy ourselves to be, because our behavior is being pulled by seven unseen strings.

The next time you find yourself engrossed in a game of golf, or craving a specific food, or focusing like mad to meet a deadline at work, ask yourself: What's actually going on here? Underneath the surface, which of the seven triggers is causing this fascination? Once you understand how fascination works, you might realize that your behavior is being driven by something far different from what you think.

You don't control fascination. Fascination controls you.

PART I

Fascinate or Fail

Will You Fascinate? Or Will You Fail?

The Big O

Speaking of Fascination, Let's Start with Sex, Shall We?

The darkened cocktail lounge of the St. Paul airport Marriott is a social petri dish, commingling business travelers from otherwise unrelated companies, cities, and professions. The lounge's ferns-and-brass ambiance offers these road warriors a comforting mixture of familiarity and anonymity.

In between serving Sam Adams and Kendall-Jackson chardonnay, bartenders witness the nightly routine of strangers engaged in flirtation, a timeworn ritual that often progresses from suggestive glances to the elevator banks in two hours or less. Had these bartenders studied Irenäus Eibl-Eibesfeldt's research in evolutionary anthropology, they'd realize that they're front and center at a nightly performance of the flirtation tango—a series of dance steps choreographed over the millennia by the Martha Graham of mating dances, Mother Nature herself.

Whether a woman regularly quotes Carrie Bradshaw from *Sex and the City* or belongs to a society with no written language, she'll flirt using almost exactly the same nonverbal signals as other women across continents, cultures, and geographies. Eibl-Eibesfeldt discovered that women from around the globe—from craggy, remote islands to metropolitan epicenters—use the same repertoire of gestures when determining whether a potential mate is available and interested. Flirting, like all fascinations, is innate.

The Canoodling Tango

In her aptly named book, *Sex*, Joann Ellison Rodgers describes Eibl-Eibesfeldt's discovery on just how all women flirt. A female begins fascinating a male by smiling at him, raising her brows to make her eyes appear wider and more childlike, quickly lowering her lids while tucking her chin slightly down, in an effort to bring him closer. After averting her gaze to the side, she will, within moments and almost without exception, put her hands on or near her mouth and giggle, lick her lips, or thrust out her chest while gazing at the object of her intended affection. And it's consistent, regardless of language, socioeconomic status, or religious upbringing. For men, says Rodgers, the fascination ritual is less submissive but no less standardized. He'll puff out his chest, jut his chin, arch his back, gesture with his hands and arms, and swagger in dominant motions to draw attention to his power (not unlike the way a male pigeon puffs his chest, or a male gorilla struts). Like a woman's flirtation, he's advertising critical cues about his reproductive fitness.

Fascination. Flirtation. Fornication.

Just as we're born to be fascinated by specific signals from potential mates, we're also born knowing how to fascinate them as well. Flirtation is the most elemental of all fascinations, one of a handful of instinctive cues upon which all life depends. No flirtation, no mating. No mating, no offspring. No offspring, no family, no passing of the genes, no species.

Fascination isn't the same as sex, of course. However, sex does provide a conveniently accurate metaphor. And unlike, say, South American bird watching, sex is a universal phenomenon. So for purposes of making our point academically, sex it shall be.

Fascination Is a Force of Attraction

This force of attraction heightens intellectual, emotional, and physical focus. Couples in the St. Paul Marriott fall into this captivated grip, and you experience it, too. When you impulsively decide to see a certain movie, when you crave your favorite chocolate almond ice cream, or when you hit repeat on your iPod to hear that song one more time, you're experiencing a similar—if less intense—attraction.

Attraction doesn't have to make sense. In most cases, attraction is highly irrational. We generally don't decide to be fascinated any more than we decide to be attracted to a certain person, because root causes for our fascinations are hardwired into us long before we have any say in the matter.

Fascination takes many forms, but all tap into instinctive triggers, such as the need to hunt, to control, to feel secure, to nurture and be nurtured. Some fascinations last only a heartbeat, while others last beyond a seventy-fifth wedding anniversary. No matter how long it lasts, or what behavior it motivates, or which trigger inspires it, every fascination binds with a singularly intense connection. We are, if only for a moment, utterly spellbound. Herein lies the power of fascination: It strips away our usual rational barriers, exposing our minds, leaving us vulnerable to influence, naked to persuasion.

Speaking of naked, let's check back in with our couples flirting in the St. Paul airport Marriott lounge.

At the bar, a paralegal is progressing nicely through her flirtation with the service engineer from Sacramento. They're performing their steps in the mating dance with predictable precision. Yes, it's all a bit crazy. But if the notion that you're not in control of your flirtation seems crazy, take heart: You're not as crazy as you will become, once infatuated.

The Mental Disorder Known as Infatuation

As things progress during flirtation, our neurochemistry rewards us with a psychotic journey known as "infatuation." Fascination and infatuation both originate in the *limbic* area of the brain, the part that houses rage, ecstasy, sadness, sexual arousal, and fight-or-flight.

In the book *Love Sick: Love as a Mental Illness*, Frank Tallis writes that if we take the symptoms of falling in love and "check them against accepted diagnostic criteria for mental illness, we find that most 'lovers' qualify for diagnoses of obsessional illness, depression or manic depression." Other symptoms include insomnia, hyperactivity, and loss of appetite. Ah, ain't love grand? Northwestern University psychologist Eli Finkel describes how falling in love can "make otherwise normal people do very wild things. They'll stalk, hack into e-mail, eavesdrop and do other things they'd never do in a rational frame of mind." Helen Fisher, an evolutionary anthropologist, explains that the elevated dopamine levels experienced during the rush of falling in love can drive us to take risks that might otherwise seem unthinkable.* So love really does conquer all, and not always in a good way.

But wait. Hold on. Why would our brains throw us into a temporary insanity? What's the evolutionary purpose for this whacked-out loss of control? To understand why fascination grasps us so irresistibly, keep in mind the illogic of flirtation, and the lunacy of love.

Fascination, as we've seen, is a visceral and primal decision-making process, one that's largely involuntary. Fisher says that our brains are literally "built to fall in love" because it's in our evolutionary best interest *not* to think clearly during the two-year time period it takes to meet, court, and produce a child, or else we might come to our senses and avoid the inconvenience of child rearing altogether. Tallis agrees, proposing that evolution has hardwired us for psychopathological romantic obsessions that last "just long enough to ensure the survival of genes from one generation to the next."

First Comes Love, Then Comes Marriage, Then Comes the Survival of the Species in a Baby Carriage

Most elements of fascination work at the subconscious level. Unlike the act of paying attention, which is rational, our fascinations have more in common with less logical behaviors of passion. We don't even realize it's happening, any more than we realize that we're flirting for reasons that have less to do with hearts and flowers and more to do with our biological

---

* A handy example of "unthinkable" behavior: former astronaut Lisa Marie Nowak's 2007 jealousy-fueled drive to kidnap a romantic rival (while reportedly wearing adult diapers on the cross-country drive to avoid stopping en route).

urge to procreate. Whether you realize it or not, you experience fascination's irrational grip.

Now that we've covered flirtation and falling in love, it's time to go a step further, and find out why your body is equipped to manufacture the quintessential fascination.

Orgasm: The Ultimate Fascination

If flirtation and sex are metaphors for fascination, then the experience of orgasm itself is fascination in the extreme. Groundbreaking human sex researcher Alfred Kinsey described the fascination of sexual climax: "Some, and perhaps most persons may become momentarily unconscious at the moment of orgasm . . . only vaguely aware of reality." Freud noted that orgasm brings an almost complete disappearance of thought, a hypnoid state with a temporary loss of self-awareness.* This focused state plays itself out in everyday life. Think of when you're "in the zone." Psychologist Mihaly Csikszentmihalyi describes what he calls a "flow state," and its loss of self-consciousness. "Flow is the mental state of operation in which the person is fully immersed in what he or she is doing, characterized by a feeling of energized focus."

Picture how your body zones out when you're engrossed in a movie, or mid-thought. You might stand perfectly still, jaw slackened, pulse rising, so transfixed that you lose track of time and the world around you. You might be so engrossed that you're lost in thought during a lecture, or you may experience the sense of being "in the zone" in a basketball game. Again, a loss of self-awareness.

---

* In French literature, this experience was described as *la petite mort*, or "the little death," referencing the loss of awareness with the surrounding world.

Fascinating messages, like fascinating people, have the potential to consume us as almost nothing else can, sucking us into a vortex of intensity. Csikszentmihalyi describes this in the addictive nature of flow, and "the state in which people are so involved in an activity that nothing else seems to matter; the experience itself is so enjoyable that people will do it even at great cost, for the sheer sake of doing it." Moments of fascination can become peak life experiences, calling us forth to engage more fully than at any other time, giving ourselves over to the vividness of complete and total engagement.

So compelling are such fascinations that in the extreme, only a thin line separates fascination from its evil twin: obsession.

When Fascination Becomes Obsession

Most of us at some time lose connection with the world around us in a healthy "flow state." However, when the connection turns into obsession or compulsion, it causes a severe disconnect with society, and even a disconnect with reality. All fascination creates a momentary connection, but obsessions create an ongoing *unhealthy* connection. In the grip of obsession we lose control, held hostage to the compulsive behavior. Phobias are one example. Drug addiction is another.

The Fascination Scale of Intensity

All fascinations sit on a spectrum. Some are mild; others, quite intense. Take, for example, organizing a pantry. You might organize the cans and jars in your kitchen pantry without really thinking about it. For someone with OCD, however, those same shelves can become a fixation that defies normal behavior, causing tremendous anxiety and stress. Same

Fascination Scale

AVOIDANCE

DISINTEREST

NEUTRALITY

MILD AFFINITY

INTEREST

ENGAGEMENT

IMMERSION

PREOCCUPATION

OBSESSION

COMPULSION

behavior (organizing the kitchen pantry), yet with markedly different levels of intensity.

Many people get into playing video games on a PS2 or Wii, usually as a way to relax or socialize. For some, however, it becomes more extreme. These players spend days in a room, staring at the screen without break, focusing on nothing but the game. In Japan, this is known as *"gēmu otaku"*: an obsessive interest in video games. Same activity, just different levels of intensity and behavior.

Here's a way to visualize this spectrum of attraction, ranging from avoidance to compulsion. (This scale is by no means absolute, but helps illustrate ten points upon which any fascination can fall.)

To illustrate this scale, let's take an example to which we can all relate. (No, not sex, get your mind out of the gutter.) We watch TV commercials, whether we want to or not, with varying degrees of attraction:

Avoidance: You'll take steps to avoid TV commercials. You might TiVo programs specifically to skip commercials.

Disinterest: You might leave the room during a commercial break (to get a ham sandwich?).

Neutrality: You don't really care if you watch the commercial or not. You're not going to take steps to avoid it, or to watch it.

Mild affinity: If a commercial happens to pique your curiosity, you'll watch. Otherwise, eh, whatever.

Interest: Commercials entertain, at least the good ones.

Engagement: You actively enjoy commercials. At the Super Bowl, you might pay more attention to the commercials than to the game.

Immersion: You go out of your way to watch commercials, even going online to search them out.

You get the idea.

Unfortunately for those of us in marketing, this is a purely fictitious example, since few people will ever become so fascinated by TV commercials that they experience the more extreme, darker states: preoccupation, obsession, and compulsion. Yet the point here is that *any* activity has many degrees of attraction.

Fetishes: Rubber Sheets, Anyone?

Back to our sex metaphor. To understand how things can become obsessive, let's peek into fetishes, a world in which one man's fancy is another's fixation.

A fetish is an excessive or irrational devotion to some activity or object (e.g., rubber, hair, stiletto boots, whatever; I'm not here to judge). Fetishes go beyond normal interest. On the scale of intensity, if an impulsive flirtatious smile suggests a mild

Fascination Scale

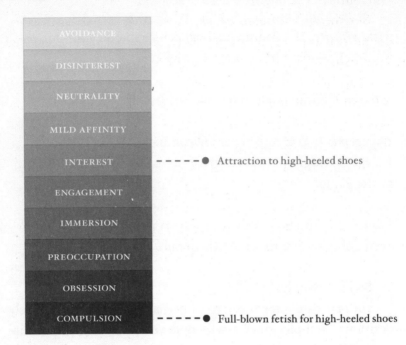

form of fascination, fetishes demonstrate extreme connection.

The word "fetish" comes from the fifteenth-century Portuguese word *feitiço*, meaning "false power." It involves a transfer of power from one source to a symbolic substitute.* Instead, the item is now imbued with far more significant meaning, almost a sexually religious meaning, so significant that the subject may be unable to become aroused without it.

Some fetishes involve commonly sexualized things such as

---

* For example, a high-heeled shoe stops being just a shoe, a piercing stops being just a piercing, and a black latex zip-up catsuit with coordinating riding crop stops being your regular Saturday night standby.

breasts, lipstick, pigtails, silk sheets, and voyeurism. Others, the sound of car engines. Yes . . . read on.

Sex therapist Louanne Cole Weston describes how even a sound can become fetishistic. One of her patients described how, in his youth, he would regularly watch an attractive young neighborhood woman try to start her car. The engine took a few tries to start, making a churning sound. Soon he linked the sound of a car engine with sexual arousal. Once he'd earned his driver's license, he simulated artificial "damsel in distress" scenarios. After seeing an attractive woman leave her car in a grocery store parking lot, he'd open the hood and unhook a wire. Once she returned to the car, he'd have the pleasure of hearing the churning sounds of an engine that won't turn over. Weston concludes that "given the right circumstances, a person could develop an eroticism for probably any sound." Clearly, early fascinations can become (ahem) hardwired.

By this point, we've covered a smorgasbord of attraction cues: chest thrusting, lip licking, even engine starting. Now, let's talk elbow measuring.*

On a First Date? Measure His Elbows

The idea that symmetry equals beauty has been rattling around pop culture for a few years, based on research from evolutionary biologists Steven Gangestad and Randy Thornhill. Their study began by measuring seven body points, such as elbows, and ended with the theory that symmetry translates not only to better DNA, and better treatment from parents, but also better sex.

---

* Authorial recommendation: If you're highly symmetrical, congratulations, read on. If you're a bit lopsided, ah, perhaps you'd best skip ahead a few paragraphs or risk a rather unpleasant revelation about why your college roommate's bedpost boasted more notches than yours.

Men with symmetrical elbow bones are simply more fascinating: they have more fun in the bedroom, more frequently, with more beautiful partners. Not only have evolutionary biologists predicted sexual prowess on the basis of body symmetry measurements, but also the level of physical dominance, emotional stability, day-to-day health, even likelihood of fidelity.

Measuring elbows seems like running one of those free Internet background checks: fast, free, with more information than you needed or wanted. But what if there are no overt cues, such as elbows, to measure? Can you be fascinated by someone's beauty, even if you can't actually *see* them?

Are Beautiful People Still More Attractive with the Lights Off?

Buried deeper in Gangestad and Thornhill's research, the data started cranking out an even kookier finding: The beauty bias still applies in the dark. Attractive people, the study found, literally smell different. Or more specifically, better. Even when hidden from view, women will still choose symmetrical males, *merely on the basis of scent*. A final blow to nonsymmetrical guys everywhere: With highly symmetrical partners, women were more than twice as likely to climax during intercourse (offering a biological advantage for funneling sperm into the uterus to promote conception).

For the less symmetrical among us, take heart. While you'll never be able to control certain fascination influences, others are more malleable. Attracting potential mates might be as simple as pulling your T-shirt out of the laundry hamper.

Forget How You Look: The Real
Question Is, How Are Your MHCs?

All those hours spent primping and working out to look attractive may be far less significant than we think. It turns out that scent might be more critical. And "scent" doesn't mean visiting a department store's fragrance counter and spritzing on some cologne.

Your MHC, or "major histocompatibility complex," is a gene family that strengthens your immune system. Scientists recently discovered that you unconsciously detect MHC genes in others, just by the way they smell. In other words, through scent, we can unconsciously detect gene makeup in other people.

So far, so good. Yes? Because now is when things get a little weird.

Scientists asked men to wear the same T-shirt for two days, without soap or deodorant or cologne, so these shirts would be nice and whiffy.* Then, in a blind study, they gave these well-ripened shirts to two groups of women: The first group had MHC genes that were the *same* as the men's, and the second group had MHC genes that were *different* from theirs.

The results? Women were more attracted to the scent of guys who had MHC genes *different* from their own. Translation: Potential offspring would have a better chance of survival because the combination of different genes would strengthen their immune systems. Numerous studies have proven that a combination of genes is stronger than a more "pure" pool of genes. So critical is a combination of genes

---

* I might feel compelled to offer more details on the T-shirts' exact scent; however, the data on this aspect of the research are thankfully brief.

that men and women with different genes experience fewer fertility problems and miscarriages, and even fewer relationship problems. That's a big part of what fascinates us in romance and sexuality: finding people with compatible histocompatibility.

But—what happened when the same test was done with women who were on birth control? A different response entirely.

A University of Liverpool study showed that women taking the pill were attracted to men with *the same* MHC genes as their own. Hormones in the birth control pill disrupt the ability to judge genetic compatibility. These scientists hypothesize that because birth control makes a woman's body think it's pregnant, women respond to men who are more genetically similar to them (i.e., family members) because from an evolutionary standpoint, for a pregnant woman, it makes more sense to be around people who will protect her and her growing baby. Taking birth control pills is a choice that's within a woman's control; however, many elements of her fascinations, such as attraction to a man's MHC genes, are not.

The Sexual Laboratory Known as a Strip Club

Multiple studies have confirmed that women are more "fascinating" to their mates while ovulating. When women are especially fertile, their partners become more attentive, are more vigilant, and engage in "mate-guarding" behavior to keep other men away. To find out more, researchers from the University of New Mexico "examined ovulatory cycle effects on tip earnings by professional lap dancers working in gentlemen's clubs." In other words, they wanted to know how this dynamic played out in the sexual laboratory known as a strip club.* The researchers found that the strippers' tips fluctuated, depending on their menstrual cycle. While ovulating, fertile strippers earned almost 30 percent more in tips than during other times of the month. However, dancers on birth control pills saw no such boost in tips. Birth control essentially wiped out these dancers' prime earning days. Over the course of a year, using the pill could potentially mean thousands of dollars in lost income.† If your MHC genes can be responsible for attraction, and the birth control pill can reverse that attraction, what other fascinations are driving your behavior without your knowledge? Most triggers lie outside your awareness, and many, outside your control.

On our journey through flirtation, fetishes, elbows, MHCs, and lap dances, we've seen how our personal notion of attractiveness is rooted deep within us. We might be irresistibly, magnetically drawn to a certain person without having any idea that it's not a conscious choice. It doesn't end with physical attraction—it only starts there. Whatever you're drawn to—from watching reruns of *Family Guy* to spending time with your family—you have the triggers to thank for it.

---

* Imagine the conversation between a researcher and a stripper: "Hello there, Kandi, you look very nice this afternoon. Those six-inch Lucite heels make you really, ah, tall. Anyway, in order to get reimbursed by the university for this study, can I please get a receipt for any dollar bills I tip you?"

† A stripper's income rises and falls with the ability to fascinate, and guess what: they're not the only ones. We all use involuntary signals to persuade clients.

The next time you find yourself intrigued by a certain person, or engrossed in a conversation, or mesmerized during an event, ask yourself: What's happening under the surface of your decision making to cause this heightened interest? It might be a complex intertwining of triggers. Or it might be as simple as a smile.

Your Fascinating Face

Why You Were Born Knowing Exactly How to Persuade

A million generations after our reptilian brains retreated to the base of our brain stems, fascination continues to be our most basic form of attention. Why? Because fascination, at some level, is based upon survival. And to survive, you must fascinate.

From the Amazon Jungle to Amazon.com

Marketers advertise to stand out amid a dizzying array of options. But marketers didn't invent advertising. Flowers did. As University of Florida biology professor David Dilcher wrote, "flowering plants were the first advertisers in the world. They put out beautiful petals, colorful patterns, fragrances, and gave a reward, such as nectar or pollen, for any insect that would come and visit them."

Plants offer other lessons in marketing survival. For instance, the Amazon jungle might look like it would be a desirable place to live, if you're a plant. It's lush, exotic, flourishing, with plenty of water. But with thirty million species in the rain forest, vegetation grows so thickly that each plant must fight to gain food, protection, and even a slender ray of light. Plants act like marketing managers: developing unique adaptations, designing spinoff extensions, and seeking unconventional niches.

If the Amazon jungle is the most competitive place on Earth, the second most competitive might be Amazon.com. Books compete to fascinate in many of the same ways, because the more crowded an environment, the more competitive it becomes, and the harder each individual must work. Flowers must fascinate insects, and books must fascinate readers, in order to survive.

The same instincts that allowed our evolutionary forefathers to hunt woolly mammoths for dinner are still very much in place today, even as we order a Double Whopper through the speaker of the Burger King drive-through. These instincts perfectly suited our cave-dwelling existence, but make less sense today. When communicating with any of your fellow Homo sapiens, remember that you're not just dealing with the person you see before you today, you're also dealing with triggers that predate this book by millions of years. Leftover survival instincts clash with our modern environment, and much of our behavior lives in the far less rational areas of our brain. We've already seen how flirtatious body language can influence decision making. Facial expression is even more powerful.

The Fascination Machine

We're constantly "reading" the facial cues of those around us, searching for signals: smiles, wide eyes, scowls, tears. By looking at just two eyes, a nose, and a smile, we can decipher and predict an extraordinary range of emotions, personality traits, and intentions. Faces are so key to our survival, in fact, that we're born to be fascinated by them.

In the early 1960s, a developmental psychologist named Robert Fantz set out to discover whether we're born with an innate ability to perceive certain forms, specifically faces. Without the aid of today's sophisticated magnetic resonance imaging brain scans, Fantz set up his own low-tech version with a simple experiment. Over his infant subjects, he cleverly set a display board with two pictures: a high-contrast bull's-eye on the left and, next to it, a simple sketch of a face. Behind the display board, Fantz then watched the babies through a peephole. What he saw changed developmental psychology.

A Baby's Very First Party Trick

While newborns' eyes appear to wander aimlessly or stare with glazed indifference, Fantz learned the opposite is true. Newborns focus on certain shapes far more than others, with a decided preference for the human face. He found that by two months of age, babies stare at a drawing of the human face twice as often, and twice as long, as at a bull's-eye. No coincidence, then, that the range at which babies can most clearly see objects is twelve inches away, roughly equal to the distance to view the mother's face while nursing.

Fantz's findings startled the developmental community, proving that a fascination with faces is more "nature" than "nurture." His experiments proved that even at birth, we arrive prepackaged with survival mechanisms to help us connect with others and form close relationships.

Facial fascination is such a critical skill that our brain has a region specifically for recognizing, interpreting, and responding to human faces: the fusiform face area, or FFA. Located deep within the temporal lobe, on the underside of the brain, the FFA drives high-level visual processing needed to distinguish and interpret faces and expressions. Building on Fantz's findings, neuroscientists can pinpoint the hardwiring in your brain, predicting whether you prefer bean burritos or chicken chimichangas. Auto manufacturer DaimlerChrysler used MRI technology to study how young men respond to three different car body styles: sports cars, sedans, and small cars. Sports cars, by far, created the highest levels of brain activity. ("What? Young men excited by Ferraris? You don't say!") While this initial finding isn't a shocker, the news wasn't that the activity occurred but, rather, exactly *where* the activity occurred. It took place in the nucleus accumbens, a deep and primal area linked to intense physical gratification. Previously, scientists thought this area responded only to physical rewards, including chocolate and cocaine. But now for the first time, the researchers watched as automobiles stimulated these mental explosions.

More startling was what happened next. Researchers then asked the young men which specific brands were most attractive, still reading their brain patterning. To their astonishment, while the young men appraised which models were their favorites, activity fired off in their brains once again. But this time, the fireworks centered in the FFA region—the region that identifies *faces*.

The link between transportation and faces isn't limited to sports cars. Anthropomorphization—ascribing human characteristics to nonhuman things—is a common way to create bonds. The more something resembles a human face, the more emotional attachment we feel for it.

Advertising frequently manipulates this response. Michelin tires plunks a couple of animated eyes and a smile onto a charmless stack of tires, and presto, those tires have a sparkling personality. Same with the Pillsbury Doughboy, Scrubbing Bubbles, and many other brands developed in the seventies and eighties.* Faces foster bonding, especially in stories for children. An early documented case of this was *The Little Engine That Could*, which used a human face on the train to help convey emotions and intentions within the story. Today, artificial "faces" bond children and machines all throughout the aisles of Toys "R" Us, from the train empire of Thomas the Tank Engine to the crew of Bob the Builder.

Would children be as focused on toys such as Thomas the Tank Engine if they didn't have faces? Probably not. Faces allow children to experience all the tank engine's behaviors, and toys with faces allow children to distill a story, internalize the message, and apply the lessons to their own lives.

But . . . What Happens If a Child Is Literally Unable to Identify Faces?

If faces are so indivisibly essential to the survival of ourselves and our species that our brains arrive into the world with an innate fascination for looking at other people, then how can anyone cope without this primal skill? Such was the case with a little boy whom we'll call Harrison Platt.

At Harrison's birth, the pediatrician declared the boy in perfect health, as he did at Harrison's six-month, twelve-month,

---

* Considering the research on faces, perhaps we should bring this technique back. The Cisco Cowboy? The 3M Three Musketeers?

and eighteen-month checkups. Yet from the start, Harrison's mother worried something was wrong. Harrison never made eye contact. He only looked at her moving mouth. With strangers, this odd behavior was even more pronounced: He hardly looked at them at all. It's not that Harrison couldn't see. He could line up stacks of toys, and often did so obsessively from lunch until dinnertime. What became clear over time was that while Harrison had normal eyesight, he couldn't see faces. No matter how much his mother played and coaxed and patty-caked, her son registered absolutely no reaction, emotion, or expression. At his two-year checkup, the pediatrician diagnosed Harrison with autism.

Harrison's autism caused his brain, unlike the brain of a normal toddler, to react exactly the same when viewing a stranger as when viewing his own mother. In fact, his brain would show more recognition for a familiar toy than for his own mother. The FFA, that region governing facial recognition, failed to interpret his mother's face as anything more significant than a random jumble of lines.

Robert Schultz conducted a three-year study on autistic children like Harrison, working with fellow researchers at the Yale Developmental Neuroimaging Program. Schultz discovered a missing piece of the autism puzzle: These patients found it difficult to differentiate between *humans* and *things*. They couldn't "read" faces to see age, gender, or emotional state. With little distinction between humans and things, it's more difficult to feel empathy, to predict behavior, to comprehend emotion, or to experience any of the other ways in which our FFA helps us connect with others. As a result, they found it extremely difficult to have interpersonal emotional relationships, or form bonds within a group. Instead of examining faces with the usual FFA processors, they lacked the hardwiring necessary to be fascinated with faces.

With this in mind, let's return to our friend Thomas the Tank Engine. In a *New York Post* article, the president of the Autism Society of America described how she'd received countless letters from "parents who said their children were mesmerized by Thomas." Exaggerated expressions and explicitly articulated feelings help children understand expressions and the meaning behind them. A subsequent study by the UK's National Autistic Society supported the conclusion that autistic kids prefer Thomas the Tank Engine over any other children's character. In other words, the exaggerated expressions on the characters' faces fascinates these kids.

Mona Lisa, and the 83 Percent Happy Smile

So compelled are we to interpret facial expressions that one certain face has, for centuries, fascinated us: the Mona Lisa. We're unable to pinpoint the precise emotions behind Leonardo da Vinci's famously enigmatic subject, and therefore continue to be fascinated by her mystique. The Mona Lisa was recently analyzed with cutting-edge software developed to recognize facial emotion. Mona Lisa, according to the program, is 83 percent happy, 9 percent disgusted, 6 percent fearful, and 2 percent angry. Over the past few hundred years, that smile has become a cottage industry; thousands of people make the trek to Paris each year to get an up-close and personal look.

Of all the facial fascination cues that we give off, our smile might be the most important. Yet from an evolutionary perspective, the human smile has puzzled scientists for years. In the animal kingdom, retracting the mouth corners and baring teeth is generally a sign of aggression, like a snarl, intended to display dominant intentions or even imminent attack. Yet in humans, this same retraction of the mouth corners and baring of teeth signals appeasement, deference, and submission. Why are humans different?

Why, Exactly, Do Humans Smile?

The smile enigma stumped anthropologists for hundreds of years. Finally, John J. Ohala, a professor from the Department of Linguistics at University of California–Berkeley, revealed his answer. We smile, he discovered, not for the visual cues. We smile because of the way it sounds. Or more specifically, because of the way it makes *our voices* sound.

To understand the smile enigma, we must first understand why we respond differently to low voices and high voices. Bigger animals have deeper voices, at a lower pitch, and a louder sound. Think of a dog growl's deep, imposing, aggressive vibration. Among animals, a deep, low pitch is a threatening signal. A higher voice and smaller size, conversely, is a sign of appeasement or timidity. When a dog lowers itself downward on its front paws, in the classic "let's play!" pose, it's making itself seem smaller and less threatening.

We see this "high pitch versus low pitch" phenomenon in the human world as well. A higher voice is seen as more polite and deferential. When we coo to babies in baby talk, we raise our voices *and* our eyebrows. ("Oooh, loooook at the baaaaby!") But can you imagine using this same voice with our boss or employees? When we want to appear authoritative or dominant, we change both our voices and our faces, lowering our voices and eyebrows.* A lower voice equals dominance. When a boy goes through puberty, growing in size and testosterone, his voice lowers. So ingrained is this perceptual link between deeper voice and dominance that Margaret Thatcher had to undergo a similar transformation before she could become the "Iron Lady." Because of her higher voice, the Conservative Party was concerned she would not be taken seriously. They trained her with a vocal coach, making her seem larger and more dominant.† In China, where a high, sweet falsetto is preferred, many women entering the job market believe that a syrupy-sugary voice will help them land a better job. The cosmetic surgery market now offers "voice beauty operations" to burn away a portion of the vocal cord, thus scarring the cord and raising the pitch. This questionable procedure creates a more "polite" voice by mimicking the vocal pitch of someone with a smaller mouth cavity . . . a little girl.

Now, back to smiles. In 1980, at the one hundredth meeting of the Acoustical Society of America, Ohala stunned the audience with his findings. In his paper, "The Acoustic Origin of the Smile," he revealed that the smile didn't begin

---

* There's a wired connection between pitch of voice and facial expression, and David Huron offers a simple experiment you can do right now to prove this. Sing a note at a comfortable pitch, with your mouth in an "O." As you're doing this, note your facial expression. Now, sing the *highest* note that you're capable of: Notice how you raise your chin and eyebrows. Finally, sing the *lowest* note you can: Your chin and eyebrows lower, in a more aggressive expression.

† If you want to be taken more seriously by triggering power, lower your voice to raise the intimidation factor, such as when giving directions. It won't make you more liked and trusted (as a smile will), but it might increase the effectiveness of your message by increasing the power and alarm triggers. Just be advised: Intimidation doesn't make your message more *right*, only more dominant.

as a visual cue, as had always been assumed, but something else entirely. "High vocal tract resonances may also enhance the infantile character of the vocalization by seeming to originate from a shorter vocal tract. Higher resonances can be achieved by a trumpet-like flaring of the tract and/or by retracting the corners of the mouth." In other words, when we smile, we pull the cheek flesh back against our teeth, and make our mouth cavity smaller. A smiling mouth raises the pitch of our voice, which is instinctively perceived as less dominant, more approachable.

The smile started as a way to *sound less threatening*, and evolved into a way to *look more approachable*. Not a visual cue, but an aural cue.

From a social interaction perspective, then, smiles aren't window dressing. You're fascinated with smiles because they communicate friendly intentions and a desire to bond. From an evolutionary perspective, that's important. Does that stranger approaching your cave want to eat you? Or to make you smile, too?

Why Girls Fall for the Funny Guy

A sense of humor, like a smile, is fascinating for evolutionary reasons. Recent studies show that women are more attracted to funny men, because humor broadcasts a rich surplus of intellect and health to a potential mate. Just as a peacock's tail and a lion's mane attract a mate by demonstrating a wealth of survival resources, so does humor impress a female. (If you're sick and starving, you're probably not cracking jokes.) Funny guys, biologically speaking, have a higher likelihood of providing for their offspring.

Funny Faces and Funny Bones

What exactly makes someone funny? Is it comedic timing? Punch lines? Rubber chickens and whoopee cushions? According to Dr. Anthony Little, psychologist at the University of Stirling in Scotland and an expert in how we perceive facial features, it's a collection of specific facial characteristics linked to our perception of others. In other words, just as chicks are wired to seek the shape of seeds, so do we innately find a certain type of face comedic.

After scanning 179 facial features of twenty comedians, Dr. Little found the winning combination most likely to produce a laugh: round face, small forehead, large eyes, high cheekbones, wide nose, and big lips. Not exactly alpha-male characteristics, right? In the *Independent*, he explains, "The features most likely to mark out male comedians for success are predominately soft and feminine." Little goes on to explain why: "in the same way that infants are pre-programmed to respond to the warmth and approachability of a mother's face, soft, feminine features put us at ease and encourage us to relax. This is conducive to laughter."

Who has the "perfect comedy face?" Using his research, Little reports optimal humor characteristics in comedian Ricky Gervais, star the of British television comedy series *The Office*. His face, above all others, prepares us to laugh. While brevity might be the soul of wit, apparently Gervais is the face.

A Smile Was the Original Social Medium

Several experts have shown that we rely on specific visual cues to make first impressions. So what happens during a phone call? When you can't actually see someone, what role does your smile play? During a call, the person at the other end can't see you, but can hear your aural cues.

Remember John Ohala's insight: From an anthropological perspective, you're not smiling in order to *look* friendly. In the phone call, you're using your smile for its original, intended purpose: to *sound* friendly.

Digital technology might introduce a new device every week, but from an evolutionary perspective, we're still the same humans. We're still constantly searching each other for clues about emotion. (Case in point: the popularity of emoticons.) In a brief handshake, we exchange a hundred imperceptible hints about our intentions and emotional state. We rarely realize it's happening, but we're evaluating these hints to rapidly form an opinion and make a decision about the other person (while simultaneously, they're doing the same).

As humans, we fascinate one another each time we interact, with every syllable of our voices, every waft of our scents, every flicker of our expressions. Some people consciously recognize their own fascination cues, and manipulate them to their own competitive advantage. Championship poker players win tournaments by reading their opponents' involuntary body language cues, and Marilyn Monroe seduced audiences through aural cues that made them unconsciously visualize her in bed. Part II will reveal why. Yet even if we're not a famous poker player or legendary movie star, we still have a toolbox of natural fascination cues. If we use our natural cues, people will join us. If we don't, they'll walk away. In the case of marketing, consumers walk away just by turning the channel.

Fascination and the Media

Trends Driving the Need for a New Form of Persuasion

The Amnesiac and the Maze

The maze at Hampton Court is one of the most famous hedge mazes in the world, and has been for more than five hundred years. It lies on a grassy expanse behind the palace once inhabited by Henry VIII, twisting a half mile of hedges into labyrinthine complexity. The maze, which looks like something directly out of *Alice in Wonderland*, also happens to be the perfect place for a study about memory.

Researchers took a chronic amnesiac to the maze, and asked him if he'd ever been there. No, he replied, he had not. They gave him a whistle, and had him wind his way through the hedges. Upon reaching the center, he blew his whistle. Researchers recorded the time. The next day, the researchers did the same thing. They asked the amnesiac if he'd ever been to the maze, to which his reply was no. Off they sent him again with the whistle, and they timed the speed with which he reached the center.

Day after day, same thing. Again they asked if he'd ever

been to the maze, again the reply was no. Again they timed how long it took him to reach the center.

Though the patient had no recollection of his time in the maze, something strange happened. Each time the patient made his way through the maze, he did it differently. Specifically, he did it *faster*. Without actively remembering the maze, he was subconsciously learning. Over time, he built up a mental schema of the labyrinth.

Memory, the scientists learned, works whether we realize it or not. All day, we passively take in messages from the world around us, even if we're not overtly conscious of those messages. Enough messages, drilled in over decades, will eventually shape our actions. It's inefficient, but for several decades in the twentieth century, it's how advertising worked. Like the amnesiac in the maze, we passively absorbed brand messages, cumulatively, over the course of years, without realizing it.

Amnesiac Consumers

It's appropriate that Phil Cowdell described this story to me, since Cowdell is an expert at showing "amnesiacs" (consumers) how to remember their way through the "maze" (the media landscape). As CEO at Mindshare North America, Cowdell creates marketing messages for clients who don't want their consumers to wander aimlessly through twists and turns, listlessly absorbing messages.

As Cowdell describes, "The traditional advertising model was built upon this principle of passively absorbing information, slowly ingraining and embedding it. The greater the number of messages, and the higher the exposure to those messages, the more valuable the brand, and the more ubiquitous."

Now a marketer's job is more difficult, because the hedge maze changes every day.

Rather than ranting about the obsolescence of repeatedly drilling in irrelevant messages, let's pause to ask: Why did that model ever work in the first place?

Papyrus Print Ads

Advertising started with the Egyptians, who used papyrus to make sales messages and posters.* In the early twentieth century, advertisers developed tools to get attention on behalf of brands. These tools, such as radio ads, billboards, and the like, were rational, grounded in repetition and awareness. They were based on how often someone heard a message, rather than on how intriguing that message was.

This model was all well and good, and during the next few decades it spurred many wonderful advertising industry classics such as radio commercials, magazine ads, and the three-martini lunch. There were only three networks, and little distraction to take you away from Palmolive ads on the soap operas. In many situations, advertising was the most fascinating show in town. What happened since then? Why is attention now in such short supply?

Trends Driving All the Distraction

Children get attention when they scream in the candy aisle. Don't Walk signs get our attention when they flash on and off. Marketers get our attention when they offer a discount

---

* I'm curious. Instead of putting posters of the sides on buses, as we do now, did they put them on the sides of chariots?

coupon, or buy TV ads during the Super Bowl, or advertise a two-for-one sale. Yet while bells and whistles and gimmicks might work (maybe), they rarely lead to lasting emotional connection, or long-term behavioral change. Interest is not enough. Neither is awareness, intent to purchase, or having share-of-mind, or any of the other jargon thrown into Power-Point slides. It's not even enough to make a better product, or to grab more attention. Like the plants in the Amazon and the books on Amazon.com, an increasingly distracted consumer demands a more powerful form of connection. Here's why.

An Overload of Distracting Choices

Stimulation is plentiful. Too plentiful. We're drowning in You-Tube videos, LinkedIn requests, iPhone apps. In the detergent aisle, we choose from forty-one varieties of Tide. On Netflix, we scroll through seventy thousand titles. On search engines, we can face up to one hundred million results from a single search. Every decision forces us to make choices, and with each of those choices comes stress. Consumers feel bombarded with too many marketing messages, with too many options and too little time.

To see how rapidly it's all changing, let's take a look back . . . all the way to 1997. It was this year that J. C. Herz brought us the book *Joystick Nation: How Videogames Ate Our Quarters, Won Our Hearts, and Rewired Our Minds.* Herz declared, "Videogames are perfect training for life in fin-de-siècle America, where daily existence demands the ability to parse sixteen kinds of information being fired at you simultaneously from telephones, televisions, fax machines, pagers, personal digital assistants, voice messaging systems, postal delivery, office e-mail, and the Internet . . . those to the joystick born have a built-in advantage." Stop and think for a moment. These words were published in 1997. If those early days demanded "the ability to parse sixteen kinds of information being fired at you simultaneously," how many kinds of information are being fired at you today? How many are you firing?

The Rise of the ADD World

In our chaotic world, our minds and our lives have become so cluttered that we rarely focus on just one thing at any given time. We've thrown open the doors to the short-attention-span theater, and now the show parades around us at a rate of five thousand marketing messages per day, faster than FedEx, louder than Kanye West, bigger than Disney World. Our attention spans are shrinking at a rate inverse to the growing number of distractions. A hundred years ago, our attention span averaged twenty minutes: one minute for each year of age, up until age twenty. Things were slower on the farm, with fewer distractions.

But today, in adaptation to our environment, our attention spans are shorter. (And shorter and shorter.) According to BBC News, "The addictive nature of web browsing can leave you with an attention span of nine seconds—the same as a goldfish." Nine seconds! That's all we get before people's brains make a decision whether to stay focused, or relocate to a new topic? No wonder we're experiencing the symptoms of adult attention deficit disorder: short attention span, distractibility, and a tendency to be bored. In an ADD world, people leapfrog to the next conversation, the next idea, the next website, culminating in "oh, look, shiny object!" syndrome.

Earning Attention, Not Paying Attention

Picture attention as a currency. When we pay to see a movie or read a book, we're paying for stimulation. Until fairly recently, this model worked just fine, because there was far more attention available than stimulation to fill that attention. People "paid" attention. But now attention is scarce. It's usually difficult and expensive to convince a consumer to focus on a brand message. Attention has become more important, more rare, and more valuable. To get someone's attention, now a marketer must earn it, often with massive effort and crazy expense.

Even if a brand *could* reach everyone, it still can't break through most of the time. People simply shut out a message by fast-forwarding or clicking to the next one.

The Ability to Shut Out Messages

Marketers have to deal with all kinds of "attention gatekeepers" designed to shut out messages: TiVo, do-not-call lists, noise-canceling headphones, and pop-up blockers. We all have to move past people's natural resistance, because now, with modern technology, people can more easily avoid messages. And even if you can get your message through the mental spam filter, you're still a long way from influencing behavior. Assuming you do avoid being *ignored*, your next challenge is to avoid being *forgotten*. (If you can avoid being ignored and forgotten, you must still actually make someone act upon your message.)

Shift from the Information Age to the Fascination Age

In the last century, information was a scarce resource. Success relied upon capturing and generating information, so information was power. Wars were won with cracked codes and more sophisticated information systems. But information is no longer hard to find. Search engines changed all that. Now, data are a commodity. What's scarce? Complete focus. Information isn't power—the ability to fascinate is power.

This trend isn't just deflating the value of information—it's also changing the market value of products themselves.

The Fascination Economy

We once lived in a goods-based economy, then moved to a service-based economy; then came the information economy, and knowledge economy. More recently, Joseph Pine and James Gilmore brought us *The Experience Economy*. Now, as companies struggle for new ways to differentiate themselves, it's a Fascination Economy. Fascination is the means by which companies will be able to charge a premium for products, command more influence in the marketplace, and build more loyal relationships over time. Rather than merely selling goods or services, or even selling experiences, successful brands will begin to charge for the value of their fascination. Companies that can help consumers feel more *fascinated* in their own lives, or more *fascinating* in their relationships, not only will win the sale but will earn consumers who actively seek out those products.

Fascinating People and Companies Win

They win bigger budgets, more time, better relationships, greater admiration, deeper trust. The ones that fail to connect and stimulate will, increasingly, lose the battle. It's that simple. You can't survive if you can't persuade someone to engage with you. What behaviors are *you* trying to elicit?

Most of us, at some point, are trying to get others to "do" something. But we can't get them to do much of anything until they're focused on our message. People won't change a preference, start a thought process, form a bond, or make a behavioral shift unless they're provoked to change their opinions or actions.

Now that we've established why fascination begets action, the question becomes, in what ways are you successfully fascinating the world around you? Is your message provoking strong and immediate emotional reactions? Is it creating advocates and inciting conversation? Are you forcing competitors to realign? If so, you're well on your way to the Gold Hallmarks of a Fascinating Message.*

---

* If not, stick close: you'll learn how in Part III: The Fascination Plan of Attack.

The Gold Hallmarks
of a Fascinating Message

How Do You Evaluate Whether Something Is Fascinating?

It's not enough to *want* to fascinate. It's not enough to brainstorm genius concepts out the wazoo if we can't attract interest and support for our best ideas. Otherwise, all those glorious little babies die an ignoble death, becoming just more pieces of litter in the world's flotsam and jetsam of woulda-coulda-shoulda-beens.

But why? Why do certain ideas captivate, while others, seemingly equally deserving, never get quite enough recognition or support?

Why Do Certain Ideas Take Off, and Others Fizzle?
An idea can be brilliant, and unique, and fully deserving of worldwide fame, yet never quite catch on. Esperanto is one such idea. This "universal second language" is simple, smart, and incredibly useful, with all the makings of a huge trend à la Facebook.

In the late nineteeth century, L. L. Zamenhof created Esperanto for the world to share one united international language. It combines commonly used French, Russian, German, and

English roots in the simplest elements of each language, with only sixteen easy rules to follow. Leo Tolstoy was one of its first supporters. In the Esperanto language, the word "esperanto" translates to "one who hopes"; Zamenhof hoped to spread peace and literacy, remove geographic boundaries, and open global understanding. Facebook founder Mark Zuckerberg wouldn't be born for more than a hundred years, but Zamenhof was already planning a language with all the transparency and utility of a social network.

By the 1930s, however, governments were actively squelching the language. The educated class discouraged its use because they didn't see the need for a common language. Esperanto did catch on in some areas, but as the language spread, so did paranoia. The Soviet Union increased restrictions on the use of the language, forcing Esperanto speakers to register with the government, and by 1938 opposition to its use was so strong that the government deported "Esperantists" to Siberia. At best, Esperanto's use was discouraged. At worst, countries such as Japan executed citizens just for speaking the language.* Death is, without question, a serious obstacle to the mass adoption of any new idea or product. (And you thought *your* idea faces obstacles to launching.) However, the threat has passed, and today's ADD world seems like the perfect setting for such a simple, multicultural language.

Yet as you've probably noticed, this book isn't written in Esperanto. The language has never achieved full-blown fascination to the point of large-scale adoption,† with only 0.03 percent of

---

* In the trust trigger, we'll see how Adolf Hitler vehemently opposed any communication that contradicted his message. His manifesto, *Mein Kampf*, described Esperanto as part of the Jewish conspiracy to achieve world domination.

† The U.S. Army has circulated military phrase books in Esperanto.

the global population speaking it. Despite its compelling origin and the ripe opportunity to spread, Esperanto itself never quite activated triggers.

The road to message greatness is littered thick with failed ideas: Sony Betamax, Edsel, Zima, Apple Newton, Microsoft WebTV, FedEx Zap Mail . . . the list could go on for hours. These ideas fizzled by never activating triggers.

If a great concept like Esperanto can't take off, what other good ideas die because they're not activating the seven triggers? How could the seven triggers spread more good ideas—your ideas—to the world?

First, to determine whether an idea is fascinating, start by checking it against the six Gold Hallmarks. (Later in this book, in the Fascination Plan of Attack, we'll start to apply the Gold Hallmarks to your brand and message.)

Gold Hallmarks of a Fascinating Message

Fascinating people and companies don't just talk at us. They get under our skin and into our conversations. They challenge and move us. They're unafraid to ask questions, and along the way, change the way we think. They earn our business, as well as our trust and our conversations. Instead of getting us to merely notice them, the fascinating ones change us in some way. A fascinating message, like a fascinating person, steps outside the norms in one or more of the following ways.

Provokes Strong and Immediate Emotional Reactions

People respond to it immediately and instinctively, almost involuntarily. Often polarizing because it stimulates a "love it or hate it" response. Examples: Bernie Madoff. Ducati. Botox cosmetic injections. Acid rap. Roman Polanski. *The Deadliest Catch.* The Bush Dynasty.

Creates Advocates

A percentage of followers become passionately dedicated to the attraction, or even consumed by it. Examples: NASCAR. The Jonas Brothers and Miley Cyrus. *The Da Vinci Code.* Method cleaning products. MAC makeup. Warren Buffett. Most religions.

Becomes "Cultural Shorthand" for a Specific
Set of Actions or Values

The brand represents such a distinct point of view that it can stand alone as a symbol for defined values. Its set of values becomes a reference point for how people identify themselves and their world. Examples: Louis Vuitton. Virgin Atlantic Airways. Seventh Generation products. X Games. PBS. Spam meats. Kashi. Fender Stratocaster guitars. Zig Zag rolling papers. Ikea. Curves fitness clubs. Pabst Blue Ribbon beer. Many tattoo designs.

Incites Conversation

The more people want to engage with, play with, learn from, talk about, and, above all, *connect* with something or someone, the greater its social currency. It almost can't help but be noticed. It sparks spirited conversations and debate among consumers, competition, and the media. Consistently "top of mind" among a specific group, it earns more attention than it pays for. Examples: Webkinz. Adidas originals. The *Twilight* series. *The National Enquirer.* Illustrator R. Crumb. *Grey's Anatomy.* Gene Simmons. TMZ.com.

Forces Competitors to Realign Around It

Doesn't chase or mirror trends, but rather establishes new standards and criteria for its category. Thinks, acts, and behaves unlike any other. Becomes irreplaceable for the audience because it cannot be exactly replaced or duplicated. Often (but not always) inspires imitators, look-alikes, and me-toos. Examples: Trader Joe's. Scion. Spanx. Wal-Mart. Donna Karan in the 1990s. Swiffer. Microsoft, then Apple, then Microsoft again.

Triggers Social Revolutions

Disrupts the status quo of accepted beliefs. Breaks with established conventions in its category, whether through minor tweaks or radical shifts. Forces us to think differently about ourselves and our world. Examples: Bono. MINI Cooper. The "Life is good" brand. Yoga. Grateful Dead. The Livestrong yellow bracelet. Southwest Airlines. John Lennon. The Zone diet. United Colors of Benetton. Prozac. YouTube. Dove's "Campaign for Real Beauty."

But Wait—Isn't Something Missing from the List?

Yes, there's a conspicuous absence. Nothing here mentions our own messages, the ones we create and put out to the world about ourselves.

That's because fascination has little to do with what you say, and everything to do with what you inspire others to say about your message. Fascinating people, like fascinating companies, don't try to explain why they're fascinating. (Explaining to people why you're fascinating is about as effective as *explaining* to an employee why you deserve respect, or *explaining* to a date why you should inspire fire in the loins. Not so much.)

The Wizard of Oz said, "A heart is not judged by how much you love, but by how much you are loved by others." The true measure of fascination lives not in your own communication to the world, but in how the world communicates about you. If this sounds emotional, that's because it is. We don't intellectually evaluate messages—any more than we intellectually evaluate whether someone's voice is high or low. A voice either intimidates us, or it doesn't. A message either does or doesn't grip our interest (and more often than not, it doesn't).

For many brands, this is bad news. People don't want to connect *with brands*. They want to connect *with each other*. Fascinating companies create more opportunities for people to connect *with each other*, through the brand. (If you have any doubt, just go to a Harley-Davidson event.)

For marketers, it's not about marketing a message—it's about getting the market to create messages *about you*. For a website—it's not about the number of links in your site, but about how many sites, and the quality of the sites, that link *to you*.

Sometimes, in such a hyper-connected world, messages become hype, losing the substance of the original message itself. To understand the difference between fascination and hype, I went straight to the expert on hyper-messaging: Richard Laermer, author of *Full Frontal PR* and *2011: Trendspotting*, CEO of RLM PR.* "We're the most networked society in the history of the world," says Laermer, "texting, talking, virtually

---

* Interacting with Laermer is like drinking from a very smart, and very charismatic, social media fire hose, and our discussion was as lively as one might expect from the man who was a CrackBerry addict before many of us even had an e-mail account.

slapping each other's backs, Skyping, tweeting, Ninging, every second telling each other things in some SMSociety. But when it comes right down to it, we're not actually substantially connected by any one thing. We are *networking*, but not *connecting*, doing things so that we can tell others we just did them. We're living hyperlinks."

After a while, that noise level turns into hype. For better or for worse, says Laermer, hype is now ingrained in our psyche. As a result, it's a little too easy to proliferate hype. "We don't stop to think critically about whether a media spectacle is contrived (as in Tom Cruise jumping on Oprah's couch just before a movie in which he plays a crazed guy), or a family celebration is actually a marketing push (Hallmark's new holidays like National Chocolate Chip Cookie Day), or a politician's controversial 'I'm running' moment is consciously put out on day one of his new book (that's Newt Gingrich). And in most cases, rather than playing roles in movies, celebrated actors simply play caricatures of themselves (like Jennifer Aniston in a movie of the month)." We're fascinated by the *hype*, rather than the message *itself*.

So far, we've avoided any discussion of Google in this book. But now that we're on the subjects of fascination and the Internet, it's time. In many ways, a Google PageRank of a company's website is tied quite closely to its level of fascination, because both measure the amount of interest, energy, and participation in any given topic. Your PageRank is, from an online perspective, your reputation. It judges how often people talk about you, how much they say, and who says it. So critical is Google PageRank that you might want to start evaluating it before naming your unborn children.

Before Asking Friends Their Opinion of a Prospective Baby Name, First Ask Google

Although I was born twenty-six years before Google, from a search engine perspective, my parents did a bang-up job of naming me. As you might imagine, my name faces little competition from others with my name. Does your name fascinate Google? How about your kids' names, do they fascinate Google?

Let's say you're an expectant parent, deciding on your unborn child's name. As we know, in a cluttered environment, the most fascinating option wins. Nowhere is this truer than with names on the Internet. The title of a *Wall Street Journal* article says it all: "You're a Nobody Unless Your Name Googles Well." Journalist Kevin J. Delaney points out that if your own name is crowded out of search results, it can carry a real professional price. No one can find you and your work. You lose credibility. And if you're job hunting, forget it. Eighty percent of executive recruiters said they "routinely use search engines to learn more about candidates." It's difficult to fascinate if no one can find you, so "many people aspire for themselves—or their offspring—to command prominent placement in the top few links on search engines or social networking sites' member lookup functions."

Having an easily searchable name is, increasingly, a valuable competitive advantage socially, professionally, and monetarily. Just as a corporate logo should be unique and easily identifiable, so should your own personal brand be, and your name's visibility is a significant aspect of that.

Google Optimization, Circa 1587

Google isn't the first inhospitable spot for common names. In 1587, a boat arrived on American shores with the first

English-speaking settlers. It included ninety-nine men, twenty-three of whom were named John. The entire settlement died. A subsequent settlement, however, survived. It arrived on a little ship named the *Mayflower*. It included passengers named Humility, Desire, Remember, Resolved, and a boy born on the ship, Oceanus. (One particularly creative father had two daughters, Patience and Fear, and two sons, Love and Wrestling. One has to wonder how often little Love got his ass kicked on the playground compared to his brother, Wrestling.) Fascinating naming might not be the reason a settlement survives in settling a new world; however, it definitely increases your odds of surviving on Google.

So what if you weren't born with a Google-friendly name like Oceanus or Fear? How do you stand out on Google, especially if you have an uncommonly common name?

Pretend for a Moment That Your Name Is David Scott

Hello, David Scott. Not only do you have an incredibly common first name, but also an incredibly common second one to boot. A quick Google yields 1,160,000 results for "David Scott." We can estimate a few hundred thousand of these belong to each of the many David Scotts out there, including the David Scott who walked on the moon as commander of Apollo 15, or the David Scott member of Congress, or the David Scott the Ironman triathlon competitor. Stiff competition. So how to fascinate the Google PageRank algorithm?

This was the precise problem facing my friend David Scott.

In 1999, David started to write his first book. Although Google was barely a glimmer in the Internet's eye, David wanted a title with a combination of words that didn't pop up too much in the search engines. The process consumed quite a bit of time, and David thought of a lot of titles, yet couldn't find a new word combination. To complicate matters, he also wanted to buy the domain for his title. Everything, it seemed, was either a title of a rock song, or a band, or an obscure blog. Still, he didn't want to require the words "book title" anywhere in the search terms. Finally, David hit upon the perfect title: *Eyeball Wars*. Two words that weren't yet associated with anything in search engines. David snagged the domain and used that as the title of the book, so when people searched for his book his content popped up first. It was during this process that David realized, "Hey, wait, shouldn't I do the same thing with *my own* name?" Under the name David Scott, he was a small fish in a big pond. But then he typed in his full name: David Meerman Scott. And voilà, he became a one-and-only.

David Meerman Scott is an online marketing and PR expert, speaker, and best-selling author of *The New Rules of Marketing & PR* and *World Wide Rave*. He describes in an interview, "Looking back, adding my middle name was probably one of the most important decisions I've ever made. Professionally, everyone knows me by David Meerman Scott. My whole business is predicated on that one decision." If your name is John Smith or Joe Johnson, what to do? Modify it. "Don't underestimate the importance of your name being easily found on the first page of search results. It's essential."

So now you know about persuading Google. But we want to persuade others, too. We want to persuade co-workers to pitch in on a project, or convince a new business prospect to meet, or raise money for a class trip to Washington, D.C. That has less to do with PageRank, and more to do with a different type of scoring system. Specifically, the F Score.

How Fascinating Are You?

Applying Fascination to Your Personality and Brand

Who Is the Most Fascinating Person in the Room?
I am facing a large room full of several hundred people, each looking intently at me. As the keynote speaker at a conference, I'm standing onstage in one of those vast hotel conference rooms, the kind with dozens of huge crystal chandeliers as far as the eye can see. Each participant in the conference has just taken the fascination personality test, and the results will give the "F Score," an overall score of fascination level. Now standing, the participants wait to hear what their results mean.

They want to score highly, sometimes even jockeying for position vying to be more fascinating than their colleagues. That's only natural. People want to be the "most fascinating" in the same way they might want to be "most handsome" or "most intelligent." In some ways, they're correct: A strong F score is a very good thing, indeed. Yet an ultra-high F score also carries certain risks. *More*, this audience will soon witness, is not automatically *better*.

F Scores: The Fascination Personality Test

My team and I developed the F Score to objectively evaluate the level of fascination generated by a product, brand, or idea. It can test individual messages, such as a product's packaging or a television commercial, or it can test a holistic message, such as a product launch. More interesting, it also can test personalities.

The F Score isn't intended to be rigidly definitive—nothing about fascination is—but it does offer a clear probability about whether someone has a force of attraction behind his or her personality. The test also can point out unrecognized patterns, strengths, and characteristics within a person's behavior, and ways in which that person evokes a positive or negative response from others (sometimes intentionally, but usually not). I've given this test at many types of organizations, for pharmaceutical reps as well as marketing executives and real estate brokers, and the bell curve of scores is almost always the same: the majority cluster in the middle, with a small percentage of exceptionally high- or low-scoring personalities.[*]

High-Scoring Personalities

Fascinating brands have an extraordinary ability to influence behavior, and the same is true of personalities. Those with a high F Score can sway opinion and action far more effectively than those with a low F Score, because they use triggers with unusual vividness and intensity. They get their message across.

These personalities might be the center of attention, or they could avoid the spotlight. They might be charismatic, or they

---

[*] High and low scorers are polar opposite personality types. Before the test even begins, it's clear that they interact differently with the world around, from body language and style of dress to how they socialize, to where they sit in the room.

might be introverted. What all high scorers share is an ability to persuade others by eliciting an intellectual, emotional, and physical response.

We don't have to *try* to watch high scorers. We almost can't help it. They're the rock stars, the media figures, the villains, the challengers. Yet their gifts are not without potential controversy.

Is More Fascinating Always Better?

In Part I, we saw that fascination operates on a spectrum, from delicate to intense, and in the extreme, healthy behavior turns into something darker, more eccentric, even dangerous. For the same reasons, a high F Score isn't the same as *likability* (an agreeable character and appealing personality), or *respect* (earned esteem or admiration). Here's why.

Fascination Versus Likability

A person doesn't have to be *likable* to be fascinating. Those with the highest F Scores can be well regarded, and even adored. However, some are intensely unappealing, racking up a high F Score because they escalate their power or alarm triggers in the extreme: Charles Manson, Ted Bundy, Osama bin Laden.

Fascination Versus Respect

A company that is *respected* isn't necessarily fascinating. An eBay seller can have a perfect 100 percent satisfaction score and sell the highest quality of goods, and still go out of business. A high school graduate can have 1600 SAT scores and not be accepted into Stanford if the application essay fails to sway the dean of admissions. An attorney can be the keenest legal mind, esteemed by every judge, and still fail to attract clients.

Famous High-Scorers

Celebrities successfully capitalize on their high F Score, exaggerating one or more of their triggers. Would Angelina Jolie be as sexy with a tamer use of the lust trigger, or as intriguing without mystique? Probably not. (And let's not forget her bad-girl side, the one that wore a vial of ex-husband Billy Bob Thornton's blood around her neck. Yep, that's vice for you.) Shock jock Howard Stern wouldn't be as shocking without his use of the alarm trigger, knocking listeners off-kilter and causing that "did he seriously just say that?" reaction. Then there's Rush Limbaugh, about whom the *New York Times* wrote, "The fact that he purposely antagonizes people is part of the draw." Finally consider Dr. Laura Schlessinger, the conservative commentator, who attracts millions of viewers as well as truckloads of hate mail. And with fame comes not only hate mail but also tabloid covers. Think of Kim Kardashian, Kathy Griffin, Hugh Hefner.

Commentators, journalists, and talk show hosts have to be fascinating, or they won't have an audience: Arianna Huffington, Bill O'Reilly, Glenn Beck, Sean Hannity. No one tunes in for tame opinions.

Politicians can earn tremendous support from one group, and denunciation from others: Sarah Palin. Rudy Giuliani. Ann Coulter. Reverend Al Sharpton. Al Franken. In fashion, think of larger-than-life personalities such as Isaac Mizrahi, Betsey Johnson, or Tom Ford. Business leaders such as Richard Branson and Warren Buffett. Musicians such as Madonna, Eminem, Kurt Cobain, Keith Richards, and Sean Combs. The sports world brings us Dennis Rodman, Kobe Bryant, John McEnroe, Barry Bonds, and Andre Agassi.

Ultra-Scoring Personalities

Consider the personalities I just mentioned above, from the worlds of sports, business, music, and media. They're fascinating, very. They command tremendous interest and, often, influence. But is every single person on that list admired? Trusted? Inspirational? Loved? . . . Hmm. Not always. Not with the most extreme personalities.

Meet the ultra-scorers: people with exceedingly high F scores. In either case, they are very, very fascinating, and not always in a good way. They're "love 'em or hate 'em" types, earning both attention *and* resentment, admiration *and* ridicule. At their best, they develop the rare charisma necessary to unite corporations and nations. At their worst, they hit nerves and step on toes, lobbing interpersonal firebombs and torching relationships.

People with the highest F Scores often earn our attention with their *lack* of propriety, values, or common sense. Role models become *more* fascinating when they collapse. The villain is more fascinating than the hero. Good news can't even get out the door without being trampled by scandal, exposé, and other skeletons tumbling out of the closet. The press knows it, too. Journalists wield a barbed hook, and we love to "read all about it." *New Yorker* journalist Janet Malcolm once remarked that journalism's purpose is to serve the fascination of "society's fundamental and incorrigible nosiness." We all love a good Page Six. Men bite dogs when politicians announce they're gay, televangelists admit to affairs, and CEOs are caught stealing from the cookie jar.

Why are we enthralled by such unsavory exploits? Remember, fascination lives in your less rational side, the one that's more instinctive than intellectual. It's not always earned with etiquette, and it doesn't play by the usual social rules. We're fascinated by the ways in which ultra-scorers manipulate the three most conflict-ridden triggers: alarm, power, and vice.

But enough with the extremists. Most organizations have a sizable percentage of low-scoring personalities, so let's understand this group as well.

Low-Scoring Personalities

Personalities with a low F Score tend to avoid extremes, and avoid volatility. These folks shine in a supporting role and often make wonderful friends because they're people pleasers. They're more stable and consistent. We rely on them, often for qualities such as integrity and comfort. They typically shy away from the power, alarm, and vice triggers, feeling less comfortable with control or controversy.

So what's wrong with these qualities, necessarily? Where's the liability? Not everyone wants to be the high-scoring type, right?

A low F Score isn't a problem . . . unless someone wants to influence decisions and behavior. For anyone with a product to sell, or a message to communicate, or a relationship to enrich, a low F Score can hinder connection. Because they don't particularly enjoy standing out, low scorers can easily get lost in the crowd, and rarely command a great deal of influence.

But there's a bigger problem.

We like to think that goodness triumphs for its own virtue, that we'll be recognized for our achievements, that our best efforts will be fairly rewarded. We grew up being told, "Build a better mousetrap, and the world will beat a path to your door." In reality, things can be a bit different. It's not enough to have a better product, or better performance, if nobody notices or cares.

Before we can close any type of sale, we must first get through the door. In today's environment, it takes a strong F Score to open that door. Once we're through the door, *then* our product can do the talking. Beyond sales, this is true for any situation in which we're competing with other conflicting messages.

We learned this earlier: The more distracted an environment, the more essential fascination becomes. Today, clients are distracted, bosses are distracted, spouses are distracted, third-grade teachers are distracted.

Now, back to my speech, and the hundreds of people who have been standing patiently during the time you were reading this discourse on higher- and lower-scoring personalities. "All right," I say to the group. "Let's find out who is the most fascinating person in this room."

"If your score is in the lowest range, please sit down." Only one person sits down: a shy-looking young woman in an unassuming brown shirt. A sympathetic murmur flutters around her, as though she just confessed a personal failure. Her name tag reads MARGARET, and since many of these people in this audience work in the same professional community, I ask the audience, "Who here knows Margaret? How would you describe her?" The answers gush forth immediately: "A real sweetheart." "Generous." "Good listener." "Great friend." Margaret, it seems, is the friend we'd all call in the middle of the night when stranded with a flat tire. And this isn't uncommon with people who score low on the fascination scale.

Continuing the exercise, I ask people to sit, based on their score. "If your score is in the middle range, please sit." Another crop of people sit, and like Margaret, this group generally includes those with fairly mild-mannered body language and unobtrusive style. The next group to sit demonstrates slightly stronger body language and manner. And so on. People smile as they look around, enjoying this personality test. The exercise continues until we have only those who've scored highest: the most fascinating among the crowd. This is a small group, but each person has a certain intensity in stance and expression.

And finally we have our winner, the person scoring the highest: a redhead named Erik, with piercing blue eyes, a tightly wound stance, and a mischievous smile. A thirtysomething Dennis the Menace. From the smiles and buzz of conversation, I can tell people in the audience know Erik (and for better or worse, find him fascinating as well).

Margaret and Erik sit at opposite ends of the fascination spectrum: Margaret is unassuming and gentle, and probably goes out of her way not to upset others. By her own admission, she's rarely the center of attention. Erik, on the other hand, is a jumper cable of energy, ferociously creative, a high-profile leader, and, I imagine, more than a bit polarizing.

I invite Erik onstage, and he bounds up the steps. "How are you fascinating at the office?" I ask. He replies, with a dry twinkle, "I make people cry." (And as the crowd laughed, it became clear from their reaction that there was truth in the jest.) Fascinating, indeed. When I comment that he doesn't exactly strike me as the type to give out hugs, he retorts: "No, because my lawyer told me I wasn't allowed to do that anymore." The entire conference applauds at the sheer audacity of this comment, shocked and delighted and above all *fascinated* that he would say such a thing. Their wide-eyed grins all seem to say, "Wow! Can you even imagine?" I'm smiling, too. Because Erik has just perfectly proven my point: Fascination is a double-edged sword.

Are you an Erik? Or are you a Margaret? How could you combine the best of both personalities? To learn more about your own F score, take a sample test at www.SallyHogshead. com/FScore.

In the last section, we looked at potential ways to evaluate whether or not something is fascinating, with the Gold Hallmarks of a Fascinating Message:

- Provokes Strong and Immediate Emotional Reactions
- Creates Advocates
- Becomes "Cultural Shorthand" for a Specific Set of Actions or Values
- Incites Conversation
- Forces Competitors to Realign Around It
- Triggers Social Revolutions

Personalities live within relationships, so the guideposts are similar, yet a bit more people-oriented. The following questions will help you start to think about your potential F Score results.

How Much Do People Naturally Talk About You, or Gravitate to You?

Do others make efforts to increase their sense of connection to you? Are they willing to go to great lengths to talk with you, listen to you, engage with you? If you're a company, do they spend time on your website, and read your materials?

How Much Appetite Is There for Your Ideas and Opinions?

More than you can supply? Are people interested in what you're thinking and doing? Fascinating people generate a lot of curiosity about what they're doing now, and what they'll do next. (Would anyone write a biography about you?)

What Kind of Response Do You Elicit with Your Words, Actions, or Ideas?

Are you provocative enough to generate a spirited discussion, or even heated controversy? Fascinating people elicit intense emotional reactions from others. This response can be positive or negative. It can be intentional or not.

Do You Prompt Others to Think in New Ways?

The most fascinating people disrupt usual ways of thinking. There are many ways to do so, from the whimsical to the terrifying. But all fascinating people reveal a different way to think, and if they can absorb our focus, they have the capacity to change our opinions.

How Often Do Others Imitate You in Their Behavior, Ideas, or Technique?

Imitation isn't just flattery. It's a signal that you're setting a standard of some sort. Fascinating people and things become a sort of "shorthand" for bigger values. Are you a symbol for anything? Would someone ever use you as a reference point when describing something else?

Not Fascinating Yet? Don't Panic, You're on the Road

Different people embody different types of fascination. That's a good thing. There's no one "right" way to fascinate. And personalities that might seem closed off at work can often blossom in other contexts or pursuits. Over the long run, shy or low-key personalities can be as fascinating as the most charismatic ones, especially if they trigger trust. Trust is the most powerful trigger in relationships, and the low F Score group often earns more trust than their high F Score counterparts. They're not leading an agenda, or distracting people with their triggers.

The point is never for one personality type to magically transform into another, but rather to maximize existing strengths and remove barriers to communication. For instance, Margaret could learn to articulate her ideas more expressively in meetings, or initiate conversations more frequently with friends, thereby increasing her power trigger. Erik could decelerate his extreme use of the power trigger by adding trust, creating a more consistent style of interaction.

Even for the highest-scoring types, the goal should never be to be fascinating for the sake of being fascinating. *Zen and the Art of Motorcycle Maintenance* says, "Any effort that has self-glorification as its final endpoint is bound to end in disaster." In his best seller *Good to Great*, Jim Collins points out that inflated self-importance can interfere with the success of your product or organization. Personalities that are both strong *and* effective focus their efforts on making their message, and their teams, more fascinating.

Do you lead? Only if you are able to fascinate others to follow you and your vision. Because, as Peter Drucker said, "The only definition of a leader is someone who has followers." No fascination, no followers. It's a fact in leadership, on Twitter, and in your own life.

Of course, all the fascination in the world doesn't matter if you don't have something worthwhile to say. *What* you're saying is still more important than *how* you're saying it. No matter how *important* your message, it still must be heard in order to be effective.

That's where the seven triggers come in: lust, mystique, alarm, prestige, power, vice, and trust. Each trigger is a world unto itself, each with invisible behavioral tripwires and reflexes. Once we identify the forces behind each trigger, you'll see why you're convinced by some leaders (but not others), why you take some unwise risks (even though you know full well you shouldn't), and why you buy certain brands (without actually having the foggiest idea why).

PART II

The Seven
Fascination Triggers

*Meet Your New Arsenal: Lust, Mystique,
Alarm, Prestige, Power, Vice, and Trust*

There's a lot of really, really boring stuff in the world. Dust bunnies. Status meetings. Tax forms. Flossing. Plain microwave oatmeal. Repeat sitcoms. Waiting in line at the DMV. Exterior siding. Watching grass grow, pots boil, and paint dry. In comparison to, say, chocolate or music, these things seem almost impossible to make fascinating. Yet if that's the case, then we've already violated a central tenet of this book: *Anything, and anyone, can become fascinating.*

But these objects and activities can become fascinating, and very fascinating . . . *if* they trigger a response. Triggers give meaning to otherwise meaningless things.

It's Not the *Thing*, It's the *Trigger*

Let me explain. Nothing is, in itself, fascinating. When something activates a trigger, we're compelled to focus— whether we want to or not. Many fascinations revolve around things that are not in themselves "fascinating" or "unfascinating." Context and meaning determine whether a person or product is fascinating.

We all have triggers that turn otherwise ordinary objects into fascinations. We all become captivated by certain people, ideas, and things that might be totally unfascinating to someone else. You do it. I do it. Fetishists do it.

Shoe Fetishes and the Interlocking Letter Cs

Remember when we looked at shoe fetishes in Part I? We saw how a stiletto (or a piece of hair or the sound of a car engine starting) can be meaningless to one person, but meaningful to another if fascination comes into play. In these cases, it's not the shoe itself that's fascinating, but the meaning given to the shoe. Once the shoe is imbued with lust, or vice, or power, it becomes fascinating.

As we said before: It's not the *thing*, it's the *trigger* that makes something fascinating.

There's also a matter of personal preference. Different triggers possess different levels of appeal to different people. Some people respond very strongly to vice, whereas others are most fascinated by prestige.

Fetishists aren't the only ones whose triggers make them fascinated by otherwise meaningless objects. Likewise, it's not the chocolate cake that makes your mouth water, it's *lust*. It's not the gossip that makes Page Six so popular, it's *vice*. It's not your family photo that makes your heart swell, it's *trust*.

Meaningless things fascinate consumers all the time, if a brand can give that object meaning with a logo. A pair of interlocking letter Cs have little meaning. That is, unless those interlocking Cs look like this:

Suddenly those Cs have quite a bit of meaning, because they trigger prestige. In our research, people were willing to pay almost 50 percent more for a pair of intensely fascinating sunglasses, such as those made by Chanel. The Chanel logo triggers prestige. (It's not just the logo that makes the sunglasses more expensive, of course; those glasses are higher quality than a generic pair. However, quality is not usually what consumers purchase when they choose Chanel over a no-name brand of equal quality.) Think about charging 50 percent more for your product by invoking a trigger.

The Power of Branding Is to Make the Unfascinating Fascinating

When consumers buy a certain brand, they're often not paying for the *utility* of the item. What they're actually buying is the *trigger.*

The strongest brands create triggers around things that would otherwise be meaningless. Even fungible or parity goods, ones that generally have fairly universal value, become more valuable by adding a little meaning: Morton salt is more meaningful than plain salt, and Clorox bleach is more meaningful than plain bottled bleach. These brands apply different triggers, but they all apply the same principles. Triggers can take something that's relatively meaningless (such as salt, bleach, or the letter C) and give it meaning.

Triggers also bring meaning to all types of otherwise meaningless scenarios. Talking about the weather might be boring ("Boy, sure is hot out there!"). But the meaning behind weather itself can be quite fascinating. Let's say it rains on September 19. Those dark, looming clouds on the horizon have a different meaning to a farmer whose crops are withering than a bride on her wedding day. Both people would be fascinated by the rain, but with different emotional responses. They each attach different meaning to the rain, because that rain carries a message.

We're bombarded with stimuli every moment of the day, and we have to choose which things to focus our limited mental energy on. We focus on those things that fascinate us with meaning. Triggers apply meaning, and the more meaning, the more fascination. Someone else's dog might be invisible to you, whereas your own dog is fascinating, because your dog triggers emotions and meaning. Products work the same way: Triggers create meaning. The MP3 player wasn't quite so fascinating until the iPod triggered lust.

Applying the Triggers

Many people don't think of their company, or their own personality, as inherently "fascinating." Many believe they could never become fascinating. Yet anything, and anyone, can become fascinating by applying the seven triggers.

A glass of orange juice might not seem very fascinating, but if you're a diabetic and your blood sugar drops low, that glass of orange juice becomes the sole focus of your attention. A mailman in your driveway becomes riveting if you're waiting for college acceptance letters. Your odometer becomes more gripping as soon as you see the flashing blue lights of a police car in your rearview mirror. A bottle of water snaps your attention after you've just competed in a habanero chile–eating contest. A plain black Gap T-shirt isn't terribly fascinating, but it sure is when Sharon Stone wears it to the Oscars. The person making polite conversation at the cocktail mixer might not be fascinating, at least not until you find out he's the CMO of that company where you want to work. The context creates triggers, and presto! You're fascinated.

In these examples, the mailman, the bottle of water, and the Gap T-shirt weren't intrinsically fascinating. A combination of triggers around them made them fascinating. Understanding how to switch on that response mechanism in others gives us the power to change people's opinions and behavior.

Exact fascinations can vary over time. But there are universal truths in fascination. Wicked behavior shocks us, loud noises alert us, and unsolved mysteries send us on fact-finding missions for resolution. It all comes down to the same seven triggers. But how? How do these triggers cause us to fixate, sometimes irrationally so?

The Instruction Manual for Decision Making

Once you understand how the triggers turn otherwise meaningless things into intense captivations, you'll realize how fascination directs decision making. In upcoming pages, we'll explore the behavioral, physiological, and psychological

TRIGGERS	Lust	Mystique	Alarm
DEFINITION	Anticipation of pleasure	Unanswered questions	Threat of immediate consequence
I AM FASCINATED BY IT BECAUSE..	Craving is the anticipation of pleasure	Mystique makes me want to solve the puzzle	Alarm demands a response *now*

Prestige	Power	Vice	Trust
Symbols of rank and respect	Command over others	Rebellion against rules	Certainty and reliability
Prestige earns status, respect, and admiration	Power controls	Vice tempts me with "forbidden fruit"	Trust comforts me because I can rely on it

explanations for *how* and *why* we're gripped. To begin, above is a snapshot preview. In this chart you'll see the definition for each trigger, and the reason it fascinates.

Each trigger adds a different type of energy to your message. Alarm adds a sense of adventure, or immediacy, or even danger. Mystique adds curiosity. Power adds respect or fear. Vice adds irreverence. And then there's lust. Ah, lust. So what does lust add? Quite a bit, as it turns out.

Lust

Why We're Seduced by the Anticipation of Pleasure

Her voice has been described as "cotton candy, smoke, wind, lollipops and velvet." "Champagne lava." "The slow folding and unfolding of a pink cashmere sweater."

Psychologist David Huron uses a different word to describe Marilyn Monroe's famous voice: "wet."

"When we see something we want to eat, when we receive praise, and even when we hug our children, our mouths literally water," says Huron, professor of music and head of the Cognitive and Systematic Musicology Laboratory in the School of Music at Ohio State University, in a series of interviews. In any type of pleasure state, our mouths produce more saliva. Our tongue moves more fluidly within the mucous membranes of our mouth, creating what Huron calls "oral wetness cues."

Oral wetness is a subtle and involuntary reflex; however, it broadcasts our emotional state by causing distinct change in timbre of voice. "Oral wetness offers an unspoken invitation to move closer," says Huron. "It says, 'Hey, over here, something good is going on. Want to join me?' We become fascinated by the prospect of moving closer and sharing that experience."

Marilyn Monroe's wet voice communicated pleasure and openness. Her voice was also "aspirated," says Huron, meaning that she increased the amount of air through her vocal cords when speaking, almost like whispering. We all aspirate our voices when we're murmuring to a person right next to us. Yet Marilyn manipulated her wetness cues as part of her brand image. She communicated with a "pillow talk" effect even while onstage, speaking as though physically intimate with each person in the audience. (Cue your mental replay of her aurally pornographic masterpiece, "Happy Birthday, Mr. President.")

Whether we realize it or not, our own oral wetness announces our positive or negative emotional state to the world. These are just a few of the unconscious lust hints we give off every day . . . cues that either pull people closer to us, or push them away.

What Is "Lust"?

Meet an eternally favorite deadly sin. Lust fascinates through experience: our appetites and passions of sight, sound, taste, touch, and scent. We anticipate what it might be like to fulfill this craving, and that anticipation pulls us closer.

To Lust for Something Is to Crave It

When thirsty, we might crave an orange Slurpee from 7-Eleven or a flute of champagne. When hungry, we might crave homemade ribs with root beer, or fresh oysters in St. Augustine. When we crave the softness of cashmere, or the sunset on Venice Beach pier, that craving is lust. This trigger can focus on an object, experience, or person; it might last moments, or a lifetime; yet in every case, lust captivates our desire for sensory fulfillment.

As early as the sixth century A.D., lust emerged as public enemy number one for Christian fathers. And not without reason. Lust seduces us from the straight and narrow, a temptress holding a skeleton key to fit any chastity belt.

Overcoming desire is no easy task. Major philosophies have grappled with this topic since the sixth century. Buddhism presented the "overcoming of desire" as an ideal. In contrast, by appealing to our most undisciplined urges, the lust trigger unleashes parts of ourselves that we've struggled for centuries to tame.

Lust tends to be particularly difficult to ignore because it doesn't stem from wise and reasonable decision making. As a result, this trigger is especially useful in heightening desire.

"But I *Want* It!"

At its heart and soul, lust stems from biological attraction. It triggers both a physical and an emotional response, one that bypasses rational scrutiny and heads straight to desire. We might successfully *resist* lust, but we cannot talk ourselves out of it. It's rarely "take it or leave it." Willpower can change our actions, but not our fascinations.

Facts create alarm, and opinions stem from power; however, lust is different. It doesn't involve reasoning. It's not sensible. Whether we *should* crave cheesy Taco Bell nachos rarely determines whether we actually do crave them.

If your message currently relies on an otherwise rational message, lust can add new ways to increase your desirability. The need for a visceral element, such as lust, is especially critical for messages relying upon power or prestige, because these triggers can sometimes feel cold or impersonal. Additionally, trust, which often relies upon rational information and reliability, benefits from cues of attraction.

Lust for Traditional Messages

At first, many people and companies assume lust isn't appropriate for them. Don't write it off so quickly. In a competitive marketplace (read: almost every modern marketplace), all of us can benefit from becoming more sought-after for our ability to make others feel closer to us. Many corporations, especially traditional ones, benefit from the warmth and emotion of this trigger.

In my brand innovation sessions with companies, we often focus on helping otherwise cold products feel more human, or unfamiliar processes seem natural. Lust can make people so enamored with a message that they're temporarily willing to ignore everything else around, lower their defenses, and consider something they otherwise might not.

Do you want to invite people closer? Do you want them to crave your message? Do you want to add warmth to an otherwise cold package or process? Do you want to pull consumers into stores, magnetically drawn to look at and touch your product? Lust builds the allure of this interaction.

Same Utility, Increased Desire

Lust is not about utility or function. A product does not become more lustful by adding more data to the instruction manual, or more product description on the product label. (Compare Microsoft's packaging to Apple's, and you'll see why.)

Great design frequently uses lust, especially when that design brings a human sensibility to an object, or makes the functionality more pleasurable. Rather than the usual PC blinking sleep light, which turns on/off/on, Apple's sleep light resembles the human characteristic of a beating heart. Product development company IDEO designed an insulin injector that looks like a Montblanc pen rather than a medical tool, evoking visual and tactile lust. Both imbue an otherwise mechanical utility with a sense of warmth and pleasure. The functionality is the same—the insulin is still insulin, and the hard drive is much the same—but design makes the experience more fascinating.

Let's start dipping into this bag of sensory tricks. Lust offers four pillars: Stop thinking, start feeling. Make the ordinary more emotional. Use all five senses. And tease and flirt. Instead of selling a brand simply on rational benefits, this trigger focuses on creating an experiential attachment.

Stop Thinking, Start Feeling

Lust conquers the rational evaluation process, freeing us to stop *thinking*, and start *feeling*. We might not even realize it's happening, but in relationships, the effects can be long-lasting. Maya Angelou remarked, "I've learned that people will forget what you said, people will forget what you did, but people will never forget how you made them feel."*

Attracting Clients . . . or Not

Remember Marilyn Monroe and the oral wetness cues? The rest of us exhibit them, too, including you. Let's say,

---

* Interestingly, I found this quotation as a post from Angelou herself on her Facebook fan page, which proves that you can use even a digital interface to fascinate an audience with feeling.

hypothetically, you work in sales. You're making a call on a big prospective client. The presentation is going better than expected: nods, smiles, note taking. You're high-fiving your-self inside. Your body language exhibits this confidence, as do your oral cues. Your prospect is consciously listening to *what* you're saying, but unconsciously listening to *how* you're saying it.

Now, not to be a buzzkill, but let's imagine the presentation suddenly takes a different turn. As you unveil your big conclu-sion, the client's face goes tight: "We tried that approach once. It was a major flop." Uh-oh. Those pleasure-induced oral wet-ness cues? Gone. Your mouth feels dry, your vocal membranes dehydrating. Your voice becomes tinnier, as you swallow un-comfortably. Gulp.

You begin to experience the alarm trigger, which we'll learn about shortly, with a blast of fight-or-flight adrenaline. Your listeners sense the change, says psychologist David Huron. Their own bodies begin to mirror your stress, and psycho-logically, they distance themselves. Just like that, ladies and gentlemen, lust has left the building.

Testosterone-Drenched Saliva

Not only do our mouths create more saliva in anticipation of pleasure, but in some cases, a different type of saliva. *Motor Trend* magazine described a Maserati as inspiring "visceral, carnal automotive lust." One UK study suggests this descrip-tion is literally quite accurate.

Researchers assessed the levels of arousal in a group of women, measuring the amount of testosterone present in their saliva. First, they tested the women's saliva. Then they tested it again, after the women had listened to the sound of

Italian sports cars such as Ferrari, Lamborghini, and Maserati. The result? One hundred percent of the women demonstrated a significant jump in testosterone levels after listening to the growl of Italian sports car engines. But it's not just any car engine that turns women on. When the women listened to a comparatively weak engine, their testosterone levels plummeted below normal. Smaller engines, it seems, trigger less lust.*

Combining Lust with Other Triggers
Half a block away from Artisanal Bistro in New York City, the scent of exotic cheeses billows down the street like a pennant. Once inside, it's an olfactory immersion. If someone dines here frequently and then dies from clogged arteries, surely this must be where they'd go to lactic heaven.

In the back of the restaurant glows the Cheese Cave, where some of the world's most coveted cheeses age in climate-controlled perfection. Bleu de Basque from France, Monte Enebro from Spain, Montgomery's Cheddar from England. An epicurean's first question might be: How do I decide which cheese to order first? A marketer's first question might be: How do all these cheeses compete for shelf space in such a crowded environment?

Artisanal Bistro functions like many other competitive marketing environments: an intensely crowded niche (the restaurant location), surplus of exceptional offerings (250 of the world's top cheeses), an overwhelming number of options clamoring for attention (through scent, menu description,

---

* Draw your own conclusions about the "guy with the sports car is overcompensating for something" hypothesis.

prior experience with the cheese). And then there's that issue of limited capacity (the tummy).

A blue-veined Gorgonzola Cremificato has a character- istic texture, whereas Pecorino Foglie di Noce is wrapped in walnut leaves. To survive, each cheese must stand out in its own identifiable way.* Exotic cheeses offer unusual complex- ity, often combining triggers. For instance, a cheese that uses a proprietary aging process triggers mystique. A triple-cream Brillat-Savarin, containing 75 percent butterfat, triggers vice. The Italian cheese Caciocavallo Podolico comes from the milk of wild Podolico cows, who dine exclusively upon ingredients such as wild strawberries, rosehips, juniper, and cornelian cherries. A rare delicacy, this golden-toned cheese costs as much as pure silver, inspiring the prestige trigger.

Artisanal Bistro offers a luscious version of lust, but this trigger isn't just for delicacies. Every type of sensory expe- rience is a form of lust. Right now, as you read this book, you're experiencing the texture of the cover on your finger- tips, the color of the ink, the sound of the turning pages.† Cumulatively, it either increases or decreases your fascina- tion through lust.

Scent is an underrated lust cue. Whether that scent is Joy perfume or something less appealing, it shapes our perceptions. Surprisingly, negative cues can fascinate with positive results. Lust's list of sensory input includes unappealing smells . . . even decidedly unappealing smells.

---

* I imagine this as a chorus line of cheese—one by one, cheeses that fail to fascinate get kicked out of the show.

† Unless you're reading on a Kindle or other digital-type device, which is fine, unless you downloaded it without paying for it, in which case you're triggering vice.

Mmmm, Body Odor and Vomit

The archetypical English pub has a distinctive smoke-filled scent. Whether patrons realize it or not, that scent is a big part of the classic pub experience. On some level, we expect how an English pub should smell. The trust trigger also comes into play here, because we expect this scent to consistently be part of the classic pub experience.

When smoking was banned in public spaces, pubs grappled with the question of how to retain their immediately identifiable smell. Would a pub by any other scent smell so sweet?

"Many pub patrons don't feel the same in a smoke-free environment," says Frank Knight, founder of air fragrance company Dale Air. Not to worry. The company's new air freshener offers an unusual scent: ashtray. "From what I have heard, it's because of the awful smells the tobacco used to veil, such as body odor and vomit."

Alrighty then! Let's cleanse our palates, shall we?

Make the Ordinary More Emotional

Even the most ordinary products can inspire cravings.

The word "lust" connotes many things, but watercooler conversation is generally not among them. Yet the most essential application of this trigger might live in our everyday conversations.

Trust is the trigger most associated with relationships for its authenticity, consistency, reliability. However, lust can play a role as well, infusing communication with warmth and positive chemistry. Lust can bring approachability and friendliness to a conversation, encouraging strangers to lower their natural barriers of resistance, making them more likely to absorb our message.

David Huron taught us that a blast of epinephrine stress can turn off audiences, making our mouths go dry and stomachs knot. Intentionally or not, subtle physical cues communicate our intentions. It's true in our voices, and it's true in our unconscious body language: withdrawn posture, broken eye contact, an insincere smile.

Nick Morgan, author of *Trust Me* and one of America's top communication coaches, tells me that "every communication is two conversations: the verbal one (the content) and the nonverbal one (body language)." When someone's words tell us one thing, but his body language and tone of voice tell us something else, which do we believe? "If the two are aligned, you can be a persuasive, authentic communicator. But if the two are not aligned, people believe the nonverbal communication every time."

Morgan points to studies by Albert Mehrabian, who found that within spoken communication, audiences draw 55 percent of communication cues from the visual, 38 percent from the tone of voice, and only a measly 7 percent from the words themselves. Each of these cues triggers *trust* over time; however, the cues often begin with *lust*. When we smile affectionately, touch someone's sleeve during a difficult conversation, lean in to listen more closely, we're bonding by drawing upon lust. If trust is the trigger that drives *what* you say and *when* you say it, lust is the trigger that drives *how* you say it. By combining both of these, a message is more likely to be heard and remembered. Trust stabilizes long-term relationships, and lust encourages people to return repeatedly.

Use All Five Senses

Long-term relationships require that those involved keep coming back. In order to trigger lust over the long term, continually pique new types of appetites. Not an easy task, but fortunately, we have five senses at our disposal.

For many, chocolate embodies lust. Yet to win in a crowded marketplace, even the taste of chocolate can benefit from a little boost of sound, sight, scent, and touch.

Sweetening a Brand with Lust

Not so long ago, the height of epicurean indulgence was a gold box filled with Godiva chocolates. Instantly recognizable, the gold box became a glimmering icon available only in high-end shops. Then, in an effort to expand, in 1999 Godiva made a fateful decision to distribute in mass retailers such as Barnes & Noble. The chocolates, which for the first time now included preservatives, were no longer a treat to be craved and desired. Now you could buy the gold box in strip malls. (Strip malls!) Simultaneously, ultra-premium boutique brands such as Vosges and MarieBelle entered the category with exotic ingredients including absinthe, black sea salt, violets, and paprika. How could Godiva once again fascinate people with a lustful chocolate experience? Advertising alone couldn't fix Godiva's problems. They needed to fascinate younger, fashion-conscious women, pulling their attention away from competitors and inside their own stores.

Secretly, away from prying eyes, Godiva developed an indulgent new blended chocolate drink. Marketed to trendy female city dwellers, everything about the drink was designed to embody total pleasure: a passionate and seductive beverage that would be "decadent, luxurious, and speak to all of her senses." Customers could only get it by going inside a Godiva store. The packaging looked less like a regular cup, and more like packaging from a high-end designer. Even ordering the drink itself was a sensual experience, with the theater of watching fresh raspberries, cream, and Belgian chocolate chunks blended to order. This drink would go beyond chocolate—it would be sixteen ounces of liquid hedonism, tempting women with a sinful seduction of all five senses.

Charged with naming this product, I toyed with lustful chocolate decadence: ChoCouture, Confection Perfection, and BonBon Vivant. But the winner combined the essence of chocolate in a sexy potion: Chocolixir.

When the drink debuted in 2006, women described how their mouths watered as they walked into the shops, smelling the scent of freshly ground chocolate and soaking in the prospect of the velvety decadence awaiting their senses. It wasn't just the consumption, but also the anticipation. Instead of merely throwing new posters in their store windows, Godiva earned retail sales through the sensory experience of lust. By 2008, Chocolixir was blended in 152 Godiva shops around the world. Voilà! Godiva's foot traffic is getting back on its feet.

Watching the act of a chocolate drink being prepared—anticipating, desiring, imagining it—heightens the experience. What aspect of your experience could you share with customers, using all five senses, allowing them to indulge in pleasure?

Tease and Flirt

Lust is a promise of pleasure.* It is not, necessarily, the fulfillment of that pleasure. This trigger often hints and tantalizes and even promises, without follow-through. At its best, lust

---

* The macdaddy form of lust is, of course, sex. Duh. But we're not even going to go there in this section. Well, not much.

makes others want more (and more and more), even if those wants are never fulfilled.

Art of the Tease

Yes, "the chase" really can be more exciting than the prize. Neuroscientists explored this premise in a simple experiment. They examined brain scans of monkeys eyeing a luscious treat: a grape.

Each monkey's brain was stimulated by the sight of the grape, and became even more stimulated as the monkey held the grape, ready to eat it. However, the monkey's sense of reward didn't *increase* when it ate the grape; that sense actually *decreased*. Maximum pleasure occurred at the moment of getting the desired object, rather than at the moment of consuming it. The conclusion: As a motivator, *desire* is more powerful than *fulfillment*.

The pursuit of pleasure is often more fascinating than the pleasure itself. Keeping that desire unfulfilled, or at least never entirely satisfied, is the key to long-term fascination through lust. Otherwise, the champagne goes flat.

Lust engages our imagination. It allows us to participate in the process, filling in the possibilities. As with the mystique trigger, lust makes us want more, yet once we experience the complete truth, our desire might weaken. There's a reason that burlesque shows are rarely performed in the harsh morning light.

Other triggers focus on follow-through of a message, such as power and trust. But lust, like mystique and alarm, is more about implications.

Not Even Room for a Wafer-Thin Mint

It's dinnertime, and you're hungry. Hold on, what's that delicious aroma? Wow, it's a serving of rich, delicious _____! (Fill in the blank here with your favorite dish.) You're craving it, mouth watering, ready to dig in. Mmmm. Now, fast-forward an hour or so. Plates are clean. Your meal of _____ was super yummy, but now, ugh. Done.

Here's what happened: As your stomach filled with that dinner, your lust for it diminished. Lust ends, at least temporarily, once a craving is fulfilled.

Cirque du Soleil uses several triggers, including mystique (its tightly held secrets), prestige (high-end execution), and power (extraordinary training and skill). Yet most fascinating of all is the way in which Cirque du Soleil flirts with the audience. Acrobats use a playful style of interaction that gaily sidesteps lead-footed seriousness. From the elaborate costumes and makeup, to the avant-garde aerial artistry, at the end of the show, audiences crave more.

Remember the monkey and the grape? Cirque never completely quenches the interest of its fan base, because it continually introduces new feats, and new global touring performances, to keep audiences ooohing and ahhhing.

You Heard It Here First: Sex Sells!

Marketers are no dummies. We didn't need a big fancy research study to prove that a product is more likely to sell if there's a hot babe in a swimsuit standing in the ad. Don't want to take our word for it? Read the study.

The *Journal of Consumer Research* reports that the image of a woman in a bikini will not only increase a man's sexual stimulation, but will also increase his likelihood of indulgent decision making. The authors continue, "It seems that sexual appetite causes a greater urgency to consume anything rewarding." Merely holding a lacy bra made the men more likely to seek immediate rewards such as an indulgent dessert, or spending a greater amount of money. The appetites appear to become intertwined in the brain. As the brain opens to possibilities, the wallet opens as well.

When Lust Is a Must-Have Ingredient

Lust leads to behavior that's irrational, unreasonable, and, in many cases, flat-out absurd. For many types of messages, this is good news. Critical, actually. For products that are irrationally expensive or unhealthy, or for messages that require people to step beyond their normal sense of restraint, lust can tip things over the line. Lust turns "I really shouldn't" into "I really shouldn't, but I will anyway."

Combined with the vice and prestige triggers, lust compels people to buy products with higher sensory fulfillment, even if they're irrationally expensive. It explains why there's a market for sheets with not just three hundred thread count, but fifteen hundred thread count. Combined with the vice trigger, lust entices someone to order a Hardee's Monster ThickBurger (1,420 calories and 107 grams of fat), or a Baskin-Robbins large Heath Bar Shake (2,310 calories and 108 grams of fat). These choices can seem irrational, but lust is driving that fascination train, my friend.

If your message must compel people to want something— really, really want it, despite rational evidence to the contrary— employ the factors of sight, sound, taste, touch, and scent.

IN OUR NEXT CHAPTER, we'll search into the mysteries of unanswered questions. Lust and mystique are good friends, and often work in tandem. They both revolve around unfulfilled interest, piquing curiosity and the desire for more.

To pique your curiosity, consider this: Mystique compels people to buy products they don't need, or even want. And in one case, as you'll soon find out, it compels them to pay a premium for a product they actively dislike.

Mystique

Why We're Intrigued by Unanswered Questions

The bittersweetly harsh taste is unmistakable. Several seconds after being swallowed, the taste still persists, feeling more viscous in the throat than is actually the case. As the bartender pours the liqueur into a shot glass, one might imagine a permanent stain forming on an asphalt highway.

Dozens of these shots have already been poured tonight, sometimes straight, sometimes mixed with Red Bull. Partiers at the bar are usually eager to place their order and receive their shot, and they often pay a premium price to do so. Yet once the brown shot arrives, there's a moment's hesitation before it's actually consumed. An inhale, as if to brace oneself, because this drink has a taste that even longtime advocates agree is atrocious.

The dark drink hasn't become popular *despite* its noxious flavor, but rather *because* of it. This is Jägermeister, the most popular product nobody likes.

An imported German digestive liqueur, Jägermeister has grown 40 percent per year since 1985. Before then, the liqueur was a modest seller among German immigrants. But then in 1985, importer and marketing genius Sidney Frank (who went on to invent the Grey Goose brand) came across a story published in the *Baton Rouge Advocate* describing his liqueur as a cult drink. The article claimed it was "Liquid Valium," jacked up with opium, Quaaludes, and aphrodisiacs. Did Frank suppress the article? Nope. He copied it and posted it in college bars all around the country. College students visiting New Orleans brought bottles of the potion back to schools, and spread the mystique.

And boom, Jägermeister was anointed the drink of "dance naked on the bar" wild partying. Why, exactly, is this revolting potion so popular? The answer itself has mystique: Nobody knows why. As *New York* magazine described, "for no clear reason at all, college kids in Baton Rouge and New Orleans decided Jäger was cool. Just one of those things that happen sometimes. Kids being funny. It's likely they chose Jäger precisely because its taste was so horrific."

Sidney Frank even leveraged the drink's awful flavor: His bar poster shows a brawny guy just after doing a shot of Jäger, grimacing in disgust, with a headline, "So smooth." People hate the product itself, but they love the brand. And when they drink it, they love what it says *about them*.

Jägermeister is German for "master hunter," though the real hunt is for a definitive list of its ingredients. While Jäger is known to contain fifty-six ingredients, rumors abound on just what exactly they are. Some claim it has elk's blood (most likely derived from the elk's head drawing on the bottle). Others swear it has opiates, or Valium.

Many companies, including Coca-Cola, pour a jigger of mystique into their brands. The more information these brands withhold, the more consumers want those products.

As for Jägermeister, whatever floats inside those green-tinted bottles, one thing's for sure: After a few shots, your memory of the evening's events could well be an unsolved mystery.

What Is Mystique?

Eye-catching enough to get noticed, yet complex enough to stay interesting. Revealing enough to pique curiosity, yet shadowy enough to prompt questions. Mystique flirts with us, provoking our imagination, hinting at the possibilities, inviting us to move closer while eluding our grasp. It doles out information, without ever actually giving anything away. Like the lust trigger, this trigger is rooted in unfulfillment. The magic trick ends if you find out how the white rabbit appears from the black hat.

Of the seven triggers, this is the most nuanced, and perhaps the most difficult to achieve. Mystique invites others closer, without giving them what they seek. A delicate balance to be sure, but successfully achieved, it's fascination's exemplar. Mystique can add anticipation and curiosity to any relationship, from new business pitches to social invitations, by motivating others to return for more.* There are four main ways to trigger mystique's delicate balance: Spark curiosity. Withhold information. Build mythology. And limit access. Begin by sparking an intense behavioral motivator: curiosity.

Spark Curiosity

Topics that spark our curiosity become discussed, debated, and dissected, often without ever being understood. We wait breathlessly during cliffhangers and suspense thrillers. We

---

* Yet take note: This style of interaction requires a deft touch, or else it feels like game playing. Without authenticity or sincerity, mystique devolves in to a cheap mind game.

wonder about conspiracy theories and unsolved mysteries: The Shroud of Turin. The Bavarian Illuminati. Area 51. From the Bermuda Triangle to crop circles, we're obsessed with certain phenomena specifically because we *can't* explain them.

Murderers seem to hold an especially grisly appeal: Jeffrey Dahmer. Charles Manson. Jack the Ripper. Mystique melds with the alarm trigger in thriller movies: On some level we're alarmed by what we're watching, but still, we want the conclusion.

You might remember *The Blair Witch Project*, the entirely fictitious horror flick that kept millions of fans guessing about whether it was real. The movie used mystique deluxe throughout filming, even depriving the actors of knowledge of what would happen next. Creating a near-hysteria for answers, the film grossed $248 million from a $35,000 cost.

The Queen Bee of Mystique Topics: Celebrity Deaths

Prime-time TV shows still play hourlong specials about these deaths. Elvis Presley's death (or not?). Michael Jackson's suicide (but there was that global tour in the works?). Paul McCartney's so-called demise ("I buried Paul"). Even Lincoln's assassination in the theater has a certain grim appeal (especially that bloodstained playbill). And on the night of July 18, 1969, what exactly happened in that Oldsmobile Delmont 88 that allowed Ted Kennedy to escape, while Mary Jo Kopechne did not? Surely the answers can't be as interesting as the questions themselves. They rarely are.*

---

* Picture Chang and Eng, the legendary conjoined brothers billed as "the original Siamese twins." They'd certainly lose mystique if we found out they'd actually superglued themselves together.

Curiouser and Curiouser

Intriguing people make us curious to learn more. We think about them, we talk with our friends about them, we might research them, we want to be close to them emotionally, intellectually, or physically. Products affect us the same way.

When a product has successfully fascinated us through mystique, we might ask friends about it to hear their experiences, research it online, read the manual, spend time learning about its history and process, and spend time in the store. If we're deeply fascinated by a brand, we might join hashgroups on Twitter, or travel to a conference where it's featured.

If you fascinate others with mystique, they'll want more information. Reveal that information very carefully, if at all. Show a glimpse without giving away the money shot.

Withhold Information

We're fascinated by mystique because of our natural desire to fill in missing information. If there's a question, we want an answer. "What happens next? How will the story end? Who gets the girl?" Withholding information can be a valuable tactic for any professional, but for some, it's a full-time pursuit.

When a Single Glance Can Cost a Million Dollars

Under conditions of stress, the human body responds in predictable ways: increased heart rate, pupil dilation, perspiration, fine motor tremors, tics. In high-pressure situations, such as negotiating an employment package or being cross-examined under oath, no matter how we might try to play it cool, our bodies give us away. We broadcast our emotional state, just as Marilyn Monroe broadcast her lust for President Kennedy.

We each exhibit a unique and consistent pattern of stress signals. For those who know how to read such cues, we're essentially handing over a dictionary to our body language. Those closest to us probably already recognize a few of our cues, but an expert can take it one step further, and closely predict our actions.

Jeff "Happy" Shulman is one such expert. Happy is a world-class poker player. To achieve his impressive winnings, he's spent much of his life mastering mystique. At the highest level of play, winning depends not merely on skill, experience, statistics, or even luck with the cards, but also on an intimate understanding of human nature. In poker, the truth isn't written just all over your face. The truth is written all over your body.

Drops of Sweat, a Nervous Blink, and Other "Tells"

Tournament poker is no longer a game of cards, but a game of interpretation, deception, and self-control. In an interview, Happy says that memorizing and recognizing your opponent's nuances can be more decisive than luck or skill. Imperceptible gestures can reveal a million dollars' worth of information. Players call these gestures "tells." With a tell, a player unintentionally exposes his thoughts and intentions to the rest of the table. The ability to hide one's tells—and conversely, to read the other players' tells—offers a distinct advantage.

At the amateur level, tells are simpler. Feet and legs are the biggest moving parts of your body, so skittish tapping is a dead giveaway. So is looking at a hand of cards and smiling, or rearranging cards with quivering fingertips. But at the professional level, tells would be almost impossible for you or me to read.

Happy spent his career learning how to read these tells. "If you know what the other player is going to do, it's easier to defend against it." Like others competing at his level, Happy might prepare for a major tournament by spending hours reviewing tapes of his competitors' previous games in order to instantly translate their tells during live competition.

Information Is the Opposite of Mystique

If you were playing poker against Happy (not something I recommend, by the way), what gestures might tell Happy something about your cards? You might take a sliver of a moment too long to decide on your bet, or toss your chips in the middle too quickly. Glance around the table, or talk more quickly than usual, or breathe a tad more quickly, and he'll know something's up. If your cheeks flush or the veins on your neck and arms become more prominent, you've blown your poker face.

At the same time players read one another's tells, they're also working hard to hide their own. Happy practices control over every possible variable, every nuance of technique. He even practices how he throws chips into the pile. Still, cool-handed experts are human, and give away tells. To compensate, some players wear hoodies to take away arm and neck tells, sunglasses and hats to hide their eye and face tells, and headphones to mask voice tells. In the absence of any clues, Happy says, it's like "playing against a computer."

Once, Happy played against a master tell reader. As this player watched him, Happy glanced twice at his cards. To avoid this becoming a tell, Happy began to glance twice at his cards with each hand. This sort of manipulation is called a "reverse tell"—purposely distracting from "real" tells. With championships on the line, players sometimes go even a step further, because tells get smaller as rank gets higher. "In poker, if you give away even the slightest bit of information, you're dead," says Happy.

A younger, aggressive professional player prepared for a tournament by faking tells in a most unusual way. Players tend to bet more recklessly against a senior player, so he dressed up as a seventy-year-old man, complete with full makeup. Opponents couldn't anticipate his playing style. He won the game.

Reading "Tells" Outside the Poker Tournament

Poker players are fascinated by one another, obsessed even, in the quest for clues. Since they can't look at one another's cards, they have to hunt for any available information. At the same time, they're obsessed with hiding information about themselves.

Away from the poker table, we operate the same way. We selectively reveal our strengths and weaknesses to those around us, and choose which secrets to share. At the same time, we search for tells—pieces of information to answer our questions and predict others' behavior.

In the grips of mystique, we behave much like poker players. A jealous wife might count and recount the number of her husband's Viagra pills in the medicine cabinet, in order to find out if he's having an affair. A tech company might regularly scour public records on patent files submitted for information about a well-funded startup, in an attempt to predict its innovations.

Withholding information, as we know, is vital to mystique. So in these examples, the husband and the startup company would be wise to keep tight controls on the "tells" they share. Learning from Happy, they would never reveal their methods, even after the game is over. They'd act unpredictably, to keep others off kilter. If their system started becoming apparent, they'd change it.

Raise the Reward

Poker teaches us another lesson on mystique. The more valued the prize, the more others will vie for the information required to win it. With only ten bucks on the line, players might not focus intently. But even minuscule blinks become fascinating when the prize climbs to one hundred grand. Once your message captures a high level of interest, you can withhold more information, thereby provoking further mystique. The higher the stakes, the more all-consuming the participation.

In addition to withholding certain information, we can also build mystique around a message by gradually introducing new information and meaning, adding layers of mythology.

Build Mythology

"Mythology" is the collection of stories, traditions, and beliefs belonging to a particular group or event. It can be strategically fostered, or it might just naturally build over time.

Remember Leonard Nimoy's show *In Search of . . .* ? Episodes explored mysteries such as the Loch Ness monster, black holes, ESP, and telekinesis. If these mysteries were brands, they'd have very successful case studies. These messages have successfully surrounded themselves with a broad collection of meaning: sightings, reports, contradictory information, and, of course, lots of questions.

Pop Rocks, Bull Testicles, and the Mysterious 33

Brands intentionally build mythology the same way. Rolling Rock has the "33" on the bottle (supposedly for the year Prohibition was repealed). Dr Pepper's original bottle featured a 10–2–4 (supposedly for the three main pick-me-up times of day). Other brands build mythology into their marketed history, such as Bartles & Jaymes, who built a campaign around the idea that wine coolers were dreamed up by two old guys on a porch.

Other brands, intentionally or not, cultivate mystique:* Vox vodka reportedly won't give a hangover, and Zima can't be detected in a Breathalyzer test. Pop Rocks are lethal if mixed with Coke. Green M&M's are an aphrodisiac. And Red Bull (the other half of the Jägerbomb) lists "taurine" as an ingredient, which is reportedly made with either bull urine or bull testicles, depending on which urban myth you believe.

Mystique offers a competitive advantage, even for parity products or stale companies, because mystique doesn't require a complete reinvention.

Colonel Sanders, as you might recall from the advertising, uses "eleven secret herbs and spices" in KFC chicken. These spices are mixed separately, in two different factories, to minimize the number of people who know the whole recipe. Then the company combines all eleven ingredients at a third location.

Maybe KFC's recipe is more special than what you can buy

---

* Caveat emptor. Believe at your own risk.

at your local grocery store, maybe not. But mystique seems to help people think so. From a brand perspective, it's hard to know which is more valuable: the recipe, or the secret.

Stories, Not Facts

Stories are more powerful messages than facts. They allow others to participate, and draw their own conclusions. Over time, a group's "tribal knowledge" turns into mythology, creating an unspoken shorthand for bigger events and stories.

Religions use stories rather than facts to build mystique, as do shows such as J. J. Abrams's *Lost*, and even Barack Obama's candidacy. Facts alone can help with other triggers, such as power and trust, but not this one. If you want to build mythology within your company, rather than circulating a PowerPoint of data, cultivate legend and lore. As we now know, information kills mystique.

A Very Secret Secret

Coca-Cola's secret ingredient, the cryptically dubbed "Merchandise 7X," has remained a secret since the soda's invention in 1886. The company has kept its prized list of ingredients in a vault inside the Trust Company's bank since 1925.

This much is known. From there, it's difficult to tell fact from fiction, because Coca-Cola itself builds specialness around its drink by feeding mythology to reporters and consumers.

One urban myth states that only two Coca-Cola executives know Coke's formula; however, they each know only half. The truth, apparently, is a bit different but no less mythologically lavish. Coca-Cola shrewdly builds mythology in conversation and the media, boosting our perception of the drink's value and cachet.* Executives who know the recipe cannot travel in the same airplane, because in case of a crash, the recipe would be lost forever.

Coca-Cola, Now Betty Ford Approved

More mythological bang for your buck: Here are two bits of Coca-Cola mythology not actively circulated by the company.

The Coke recipe, which originally included cocaine, became cocaine-free in the 1920s. However, the drink is still made with coca leaf, and one of the main Coca-Cola processing plants must still remove the cocaine (in a process aptly named "decocainization"). Doing so requires an official Drug Enforcement Agency permit, and only the Stepan Company in New Jersey has this DEA permit.

---

* Spoiler Alert: In the book *For God, Country and Coca-Cola*, Mark Pendergrast outs what many believe to be the classic Coke recipe. Coca-Cola's inventor, John S. Pemberton, kept it in a collection of formulas:

INGREDIENTS:
1 oz caffeine citrate
3 oz citric acid
1 fl oz vanilla extract
1 qt lime juice
2.5 oz flavoring (no further clarification here . . . could this be the mysterious 7X?)
30 lb sugar
4 fl oz powder extract of cocaine (decocainized flavor essence of the coca leaf)
2.5 gallon water
caramel sufficient

FLAVORING:
80 oil orange
40 oil cinnamon
120 oil lemon
20 oil coriander
40 oil nutmeg
40 oil neroli
Mix caffeine acid and lime juice in 1 quart boiling water add vanilla and flavoring when cool. Let stand for 24 hours.

The cocaine-free leaves are sent to the Coca-Cola Company. In a package ostensibly labeled "coke from Coke," the leaves' active ingredient is sold for medicinal purposes to Mallinckrodt, a pharmaceutical company. Ironically, Mallinckrodt is one of the world's largest supplier of anti-addiction medications.

Another juicy bit. When Cola-Cola employees were busted for trying to sell the secret formula to Pepsi for $1.5 million, Coke's CEO said that the breach "underscores the responsibility we each have to be vigilant in protecting our trade secrets. Information is the lifeblood of the company." But guess who turned the Coke employees in to the feds? Pepsi.

Secret formulas can turn an otherwise mundane recipe of any sort into a source of fascination. If mystique is the lifeblood of sugar water, consider what it might accomplish for your company.

Limit Access

Successfully mysterious people and groups limit access. They maintain control by making people feel special to be "on the inside."

When people feel that they're part of the select few, they're more committed. And they make all those people on the *outside* want to get *inside* to see what all the fuss is about, building mystique envy. Even after they've been allowed past the velvet rope, it should still be a long and interesting walk to the inner sanctum, so their anticipation builds for another opportunity to connect.

The Kitchen Inside the Kitchen

In LA, a city where very little remains hidden, one restaurant thrives on mystique. The name of the restaurant is Crustacean, and it's famous for its garlic crab dish. I would tell you how the garlic crab dish is made, but like every other devotee of the signature dish, I have no idea. The dish is made inside the "Secret Kitchen," a kitchen that's built inside the restaurant's main kitchen, where only the founding family's relatives are permitted. In between star spotting and deal making, you know what diners are talking about? The one thing they can't have. Access.

Maybe Crustacean can teach us a thing or two in our own lives. Continually make your audience, whether your consumers, or employer, or significant other, eager to learn more. With your romantic partner, who knows . . . perhaps install a bedroom inside the bedroom?

Rarity of Confidentiality

These days, mystique has, alas, become rare. Confidentiality is all but extinct, because we have too much access. We're living in a time of kiss-and-tell and tell-alls. A time when starlets race the tabloids to announce their own exposé. When companies confess to problems before the bloggers expose them. When Larry Flynt offers a $1 million bounty for any proof of a sexual encounter with a high-ranking government official. And then there's YouTube, the ultimate mystique killer. Yet this dearth of privacy makes genuine mystique—when we can find it—all the more fascinating.

Mystique Buzzkill

Someone ruining the big surprise ending to *The Crying Game* or *The Sixth Sense* before you've actually seen the movie: That's a mystique buzzkill. If mystique is your main trigger, remember, your mystique ends when the chase ends. Once lost, mystique cannot be regained. It must be impeccably maintained, without ever fulfilling the desire for more information, or else the spell will be shattered forever. If Sophia Loren declined on-camera nude scenes, so should we all.

Know when to end your message. And on that note, we'll end here.

ON TO ALARM, THE threat of negative consequences. We'll learn about positive effects of alarm: why deadlines make us more productive, and why demands push us to achieve more. We'll also learn the less pleasant side to alarm, such as when your computer freezes (and you haven't backed up the hard drive recently).

Alarm

Why We Take Action at the Threat of Negative Consequences

In the photo, it looks as though someone turned the car inside-out. Disemboweled passenger seats spill onto the ground, a smashed windshield flails from the dashboard, the headlights grimace. The car's frame, frozen in time, seems to writhe on the ground around the lamppost.

There's a reason for the expression, "I couldn't look away . . . it was like a car accident." Macabre photos are as fascinating as they are unpleasant. Organizations such as MADD (Mothers Against Drunk Driving) frequently use explicit photos in their advertising, shocking us into the reality of hitting a lamppost at eighty miles per hour. Many drivers feel so repelled by these graphic consequences that they either call a cab or stick to Diet Coke. Many drivers, that is, but not all. Teenage drivers aren't as alarmed by the graphic threat of drunk driving, thanks to an adolescent sense of immortality.

This presents a peculiar problem for drunk driving prevention. How can teens be convinced not to drive drunk if death doesn't top their list of concerns? What could possibly be more alarming than being inside a car turned wrong-side-out?

Luke Sullivan, a legendary advertising writer, solved the problem. Luke knew that teens don't fear death in the same way as adults. He also figured out what *does* create alarm among these drivers: losing their license. Armed with that fact, he threatened teens with the ultimate dire consequence.

In Luke's ad, we see a picture of a teenage guy on the way to prom, with his corsage-wearing date at his side. The headline reads: "If the thought of losing your life doesn't keep you from drinking and driving, imagine losing your license." In the photo, the boy is being chauffeured to prom . . . by Mommy.

What Is Alarm?

The sight of blood. An unexpected phone call in the middle of the night. Shooting chest pains. Losing sight of your child in a crowd. A guy in a striped sweater named Freddy Krueger running at you with a hand made of five knives. Infrequent though they may be, these situations rev up our internal crisis center. We're hit with a blast of adrenaline, motivated to fight-or-flight. Now. Now!

Physiologically, people are programmed to focus and act. Under the influence of alarm, people respond in one of two ways: attempt to get rid of the danger, or panic and flee the perceived danger. Fight or flight. In either case, they often ignore rational thought, acting instead under far more instinctive motives.

Our bodies involuntarily respond to alarm in specific ways, such as increased heart rate, decreased motor skills, and the perceptual narrowing of tunnel vision. It all translates to simple physical responses: that thin trickle of sweat sliding down your temple as you sit for your performance review, or the kaboom-kaboom in your chest when the HR department calls and asks if you've "got a minute." Something's about to happen, and the situation demands focus.

These instinctive reactions started before the modern workplace, before we were even human. At the beginning of our evolutionary journey, in the swamps of Pangaea, alarm was our most important trigger for survival.*

Eat Dinner, or Be Dinner

Join me for a walk down memory lane (and as we walk, let's envision our knuckles scraping along the ground, since this is a few million years ago). Suddenly, you and I spot a saber-toothed tiger staring at us, its fangs dripping with anticipation. "Hmm, this could go badly," you grunt to me. And right you are. We have approximately 0.03 second to decide whether to stand our ground, or hightail it outta there. Fight, or flight. Eat dinner, or be dinner.

We experience this same involuntary response today. Even when there's no immediate mortal danger, the alarm trigger sets bells ringing and survival juices pumping.

Another scenario. Let's say we're having dinner together, you and I, at a sushi restaurant. You bite into a nice, big piece of avocado . . . only to realize with wide-eyed horror that the green lump you just downed is actually not avocado, but *wasabi*, the scorching green Japanese horseradish. You have

---

* Lust is another of the oldest triggers, because it guaranteed a little procreation booty.

approximately 0.03 second to decide whether to go through
with swallowing the huge lump of wasabi, or deposit it into the
nearest napkin. Fight, or flight. Not exactly pleasant choices.
So why would anyone actively pursue risky activities?

Roller Coasters and Roulette Wheels

We work hard to eliminate mortal dangers in our environment. We sterilize, we vaccinate, we declaw, we bubble-wrap.
Given this, how, exactly, can we explain the popularity of risk-
chasing pastimes such as skydiving, or running with the bulls?
It all comes down to the adrenaline rush. A few generations
ago, humans experienced danger at every turn. Now we miss
the rush, according to scientists, and some of us even crave it.
Without the daily prospect of death, we artificially generate
adrenaline by tempting fate. For instance, that little rush of
running a yellow light? It's two triggers at work, vice and alarm.
A double-dose thrill of vehicular disobedience. Naughty you.

Not only do many people seek alarm, but most people
respond to it positively when it is applied with constructive
goals. How? There are five pillars for instilling alarm: Define
consequences, create deadlines, or increase perceived danger.
Along the way, we'll also want to focus—not on the risks most
likely—but on the ones most feared. And finally, we'll need to
use distress to steer positive action.

By more clearly defining consequences associated with your
message, you can more specifically shape behavior around them.

Define Consequences

The alarm trigger has a unique ability to compel people to do
things they otherwise don't care to do, in order to avoid consequences. Tax forms are not considered widely fascinating.

However, if you haven't completed them, they become positively riveting on April 14. How does the IRS convince you to willingly hand over a percentage of your income? It clearly defines the consequences.

Consequences usually follow a similar formula: "If you don't do *this*, then *that* will happen." For instance, "If you don't pay your taxes, you go to prison." Another example: Kids aren't always so fond of cauliflower or Brussels sprouts. Many parents (including me) persuade kids to eat veggies with this classic alarm-based warning: "If you don't finish your vegetables, you can't have dessert."

You experience this every day. If you don't stop hitting the snooze alarm, you'll be late for work. If you don't train for that marathon, you'll fizzle halfway through. If you paint your house chartreuse, your neighborhood association will get cranky. And so on. Deadlines and demands prompt us to act.

The more clearly a message points to consequences, and the greater those consequences, the more urgently people focus on the message. During a fire drill, we might be mildly attentive or bored. Sure, we have to act, but it's not mortal danger. At the opposite end of the spectrum, if someone shouts, "Fire!" in a crowded theater, we'll use whatever means possible to flee the threat.

To increase the likelihood of action around your consequences, strengthen your argument with a deadline. Whether gentle or rigorous, deadlines heighten immediacy.

Create Deadlines

Alarm is such a universal and involuntary trigger that people manipulate it for a variety of different uses: leadership, politics, fund-raising, and parenting. (And marketing, of course.)

As we saw with the IRS tax forms, deadlines can effectively persuade people to accomplish unpleasant tasks. The same principle applies in motivating many types of behavior toward goals. Through deadlines, leaders can positively motivate large groups of people, especially when used in combination with triggers such as trust, power, and prestige.

When people are getting in shape, personal trainers help them stay focused on a specific weight or fitness goal. Year-end sales quotas can help sales reps stay on track. Clearly defined agreements can sustain progress, even when things get tough. Deadlines also help sell ShamWows, Slap Chops, and Egg Genies to insomniacs.

Ginsu Knives and Exclamation Points

Maybe you've had this happen. It's late at night, you can't sleep, and you find yourself watching an infomercial or maybe QVC. The spokesperson holds a snazzy new Snuggie design, or a nifty Hang-o-Matic closet organizer. She announces that she has just one hundred Hang-o-Matics remaining at this price, so whatever you do, *call now.*

Now, let me remind you, it's late, and you're awake rather than asleep, perhaps eating a bowl of sugary cereal in bed. Whatever. The point is, you don't need a Hang-o-Matic closet organizer, and only a few minutes ago found out what one is, but because they're apparently about to all be gone, *forever,* never to be available ever again, you, like millions of people, might find yourself pausing to say, "Well, quick, let's think . . ." Alarm provides just enough incentive to push a decision across the line.

We generally don't like to lose potential options. When deadlines are applied, we're forced to make a decision. Indecision is a decision. eBay mastered this technique, whipping bidders into a frenzy during the final countdown phase of a hot auction. If you don't bid, you might lose out on that must-have Hello Kitty backpack.

Perhaps you've never succumbed to a late-night infomercial urge, but you've probably noticed the urgency in those ads for one-day department store sales ("Sale ends at midnight!"), for Ginsu knives ("Call now and we'll throw in the free wind chimes!"), or for monster truck rallies ("Sunday! Sunday! Sunday!"). These ads use a frenzy of exclamation points to whip us into a panic. These messages are intended not only to communicate a product, but also to communicate scarcity, limited time availability, and consequences.

Alarm-based marketing logic often goes something like this: There is a *limited quantity* (scarcity). Unless you *act now* (urgency), you'll lose your opportunity (consequence). When crafting a message for an audience who is stuck in apathy or indecision, deadlines and consequences overcome inertia to create action.

What if the person who's stuck in apathy is you? If you need to direct a specific action, deadlines create focus. If you're a procrastinator, alarm can be your best friend.

At What Point Does a Procrastinator Stop Procrastinating?

Ever have trouble focusing on a task, delaying it again and again until finally the deadline is perilously close, and you suddenly seem to magically snap into focus? As a procrastinator, you have alarm to thank for your sudden ability to accomplish the task. Alarm, we now know, sparks a series of involuntary physical responses, one of which is adrenal focus. When a deadline is comfortably far away, procrastinators don't feel enough alarm to merit attention. As the deadline looms, the consequences of missing the deadline become more imminent. Studies show that's the point at which alarm reaches a critical mass, and the task becomes fascinating in order to avoid the consequences.

Do customers procrastinate about buying your product? The greater the resistance to a task (e.g., paying taxes), the greater the consequences must be in order to compel us to do it (e.g., prison shower stalls). For a customer waffling about a decision, a message with alarm can tip him over to your side. Define consequences, and ratchet them up for failure to act— but stop before they become paralyzed.

Deer in Headlights

Increasing perceived danger increases fascination. However, there's a law of diminishing returns at play. If alarm gets dialed up to the point of panic, the benefits diminish. Just as the body sweats and trembles in the presence of alarm, at a certain point, the brain shuts down and we lose the ability to problem solve. Neuroscience shows that after the fear system of the brain kicks into overdrive, decision making stops. We stop thinking creatively, and start reacting purely out of fear.

If you're a manager, apply threats constructively. Whether real or perceived, alarm flings people into high alert, filling them with a sense of readiness, danger, or even terror. In the face of too much pressure, with consequences that are too great, people can't perform. They simply shut down, thrust into a frozen deer-in-headlights confusion. A manager's message is no longer fascinating if her group is unable to respond.

Increase Perceived Danger

Not many candies use alarm to fascinate. Most breath mints, for instance, position themselves as politely "refreshing." Altoids is different. It's "curiously strong," and sold in a tin box. (What? Mints in a tin box? Whoa, stand back.) The advertising revolves around mints so strong they're borderline dangerous, with headlines such as "Awakens like a horsewhip on the backflesh." Good morning, indeed.

Earlier, we saw that the higher the consequence, and the more immediate the danger, the greater the action. Infomercials and IRS tax forms might be boring and contrived; however, they succeed in driving desired behavior such as ordering Ronco products or filling out forms.

It's a simple equation: Alarm threatens. We act. Of all the seven triggers, this one is the most visceral, and never is it more visceral than when applied to the human body itself.

The Suicide That Wasn't

The Amtrak Acela high-speed commuter train is dark steely gray with blue vinyl seats. It arrives with astonishing noise and speed, decelerating from its seventy-eight-mile-per-hour blur only upon reaching the platform. It was in front of this train, on the night of October 27, 2006, that Jay Gnospelius chose to jump. He selected this particular train for its snub-nosed design, which seemed to offer the highest likelihood of instant death. Because most of all, in his suicide attempt, Jay Gnospelius wanted to avoid being mutilated.

Ten days later, Jay awoke in Yale New Haven Hospital's Intensive Care Unit. His family lawyers had already begun scouring the length of tracks and surrounding area for a negligence lawsuit against Amtrak and the station. This stopped once Jay revealed to his wife that he chose to jump, the result of a psychotic break. The answers lay not at the tracks of the Amtrak station, but within Jay's psyche. With this, Jay began the long process of reconciling the fact that he had not, in fact, avoided mutilation.

Eighteen months later, Jay introduced himself to me via e-mail to discuss marketing around his foundation. The first thing I notice is his sense of humor. Jay is funny. Laugh-out-loud funny. I ask Jay if he was always as funny as he is now, and he responds dryly, "A train can't knock funny into you, and it can't knock funny out of you." He is devastatingly blunt, and there is nothing about Jay's life—no question, no stigma, no skewering reality—that's off limits in his conversation. Sometimes this brand of shock value goes beyond shocking. His website proclaims, "When life takes your limbs, make limbo-nade." He wasn't committing suicide, he was "knocking boots with a train." And he describes the whole event as "A Night to Dismember." (He's using the vice trigger in his wicked humor, and more than a little of the power trigger for control.)

Jay's presence brings up certain questions rooted in the alarm trigger, questions that part of you might prefer to leave unasked. "How did it happen?" "Why did he do it?" And perhaps most alarming of all, "What if that were me?"

After researching and interviewing Jay for several months, I invited him to join me at a conference where I was speaking, in New York City. There, in the hotel lobby, as the escalator glided to meet him, I first caught sight of his face. Then I watched as his body came into full view gradually, dramatically. Suddenly my brain goes haywire. My God, his arm—where is his arm? And his leg?

I know that Jay has no right arm and left leg. Of course.

And Jay is well aware of the alarm his presence sets off in other people. He describes my reaction as a natural one: Our minds expect four limbs, and when that expectation is violated, on some level, it's threatening. The experience is a visual representation of consequences, like those MADD car wreck photos. Except it's not a photo. And Jay knows this. He expects it. And on some level, he relishes it.

Over the past two years, Jay has become remarkably skilled at wielding alarm. Pushing buttons left and right, Jay uses alarm to snap attention in his direction, creating compulsively must-watch scenarios. You can't ignore him if you tried, because if you do, he'll just increase the intensity until you pay attention. Jay once compared the experience of people meeting him to the Romans in the Colosseum, "like watching a prisoner thrown to the lions." (However, considering how cunningly Jay uses the alarm trigger, I'm not sure whether Jay is the prisoner or the lion.)

Despite his daredevil attitude, underneath, Jay's body is a metaphor for himself: strong and challenging with a tough exterior, yet also vulnerable and flawed. For all his titanium bionics, Jay is very human.

Superficially, Jay's story and physical differences make him a fascinating guy. But what *keeps* him fascinating are the ways in which he strategically applies alarm to his goals. As a motivational speaker and advocate for the American Foundation for Suicide Prevention, he delivers a message that is hard to ignore, or forget. He channels our alarm into action. Alarm holds our own insecurities up to our faces, forcing us to confront squeamish realities about our own mortality. So does Jay.

Every message has the potential to activate alarm. Sometimes this alarm is buried deep inside, but in Jay's case, it's immediately apparent. If we learn from Jay's approach, rather than shielding people from their own natural fear, we should heighten it. Rather than overcoming our so-called flaws, we should push them into service for our higher purpose.

Focus Not on the Crisis Most *Likely*, but on the One Most *Feared*

By identifying an audience's hot buttons, a message can target which alarm creates enough fascination to change behavior. Often, the most frightful risks are highly implausible, and might not be immediately obvious. To convince teens not to drive drunk, for example, writer Luke Sullivan didn't use graphic implications of car accidents; he used social implications of losing one's driver's license. Generating a sense of urgency often has less to do with rational threats, and more with understanding human behavior.

Many people have trouble staying fascinated by their diet and workout routine. Long-term health benefits, such as greater longevity and lower heart disease, often fail to motivate people to the gym as quickly as the prospect of an unpleasant unveiling at bathing suit season. In fact, when it comes to staying fit, the *fear* of looking unattractive is more motivating than the *hope* of a slim physique.

Similarly, the hamburger you eat for dinner will be far more likely to kill you with heart disease than mad cow disease. Avian flu has killed zero Americans, but fear of avian flu infected the media throughout 2005. Chain saws injure 36,000 Americans each year, while clothing injures 112,000 (oops, careful with that zipper). It wouldn't make sense to focus on cold facts in this situation, when people are motivated more by perceptions.

Know the "Got Milk" campaign? Of course you do. It's famous for hitting on a genius truth of alarm: We're more fearful of running out of milk while eating chocolate chip cookies than we are fearful of weak bones. The threat of crippling osteoporosis might compel us to drink more milk, but the threat of running out of milk while eating chocolate chip cookies sends us dashing to the convenience store.

Like many aspects of fascination, it's illogical. Alarm responses don't always make sense. Think back to the comparison of a fire drill versus a fire in a theater. In the actual fire, people will go to any lengths to escape the source of alarm. This does make sense, if escaping the theater is a matter of life or death.

But what about the opposite? Would an audience also begin a stampede on their way *inside* a theater? On one bitterly cold December evening, that very thing happened.

Blood on the Shoes
Outside the Riverfront Coliseum, thousands of fans waited anxiously. Many had traveled to Cincinnati for the sold-out concert. By 1 P.M., the crowd bulged for the 8 P.M. show. Patience, and breathing room, were in short supply. Soon the doors would open, and the audience could stream inside to claim their first-come-first-served seating.

Then, unexpectedly, the musicians began a sound check. Fans mistook this music for the start of the actual concert. The crowd of eight thousand steamrollered forward, irrationally alarmed to miss securing a good seat to watch the show. Closed glass doors couldn't hold them back. A door was shattered, and the crowd crushed one another past shards.

General admission tickets were known as "animal-style" seating. As this herd shoved forward to find seats, no one seemed to notice the blood on the bottoms of their shoes. But by the time the concert began, eleven people had been trampled to death, owing to the threat of negative consequences: missing a good seat to watch the Who in concert on December 3, 1979.

Like the other six triggers, alarm doesn't always make sense. But it does compel people to act, and act quickly. For positive action, point this action toward desired behavior.

Use Distress to Steer Positive Action

Often, people mistakenly think of alarm as inherently negative. Not so. Like all triggers, this one isn't inherently "good" or "bad." It often has very positive results, as we'll see. Managed correctly, creating a sense of crisis can develop immediate motivation, unite groups, and cost-effectively get large numbers of people involved. The green movement, for instance, took off when a critical mass of people became alarmed about the future of the environment. Until people became fascinated through alarm, they were perfectly happy to toss paper and glass in the same bin.

It's easy to understand why people become fascinated by alarming events such as a flood warning, or a lover saying, "We have to talk." But let's test this theory. Could commodities such as salt or sand become alarming? What about water?

Tap water, straight from the faucet, is even less fascinating than bottled water. Could tap water possibly become so fascinating that people would actually pay a dollar for a plain glass of water straight from the faucet?

The Tap Project

If you're reading this book, odds are you enjoy the privilege of plentiful drinking water. In restaurants, we can usually have as much free water as we like. Around the world, however, 990 million people live in a state of crisis, without access to clean and safe drinking water. To fetch water, in many developing countries girls and women must walk up to three hours daily. Most alarming, more than 4,200 children die every day from not having clean drinking water. UNICEF works to provide lifesaving water to impoverished children. However, the organization doesn't receive enough funds to keep these thousands of children from dying each day without clean water.

Simply asking for donations doesn't work. At least, it doesn't work well *enough*. How could UNICEF increase alarm, in order to increase contributions? How could they make clean drinking water *fascinating*? In 2007, the ad agency Droga5 invented a solution, named the Tap Project.

What If Every Glass of Water You Drank Quenched Someone Else's Thirst?

The Tap Project poses this question, asking restaurant patrons to pay for something they normally take for granted. Diners donate a single dollar for tap water before a meal. People are able to donate by simply doing something they're already doing: going out to eat and drinking water. Better, with each dollar, UNICEF gives a child clean drinking water for forty days.

What began growing one drop at a time in 2007 has since flooded to include thousands of restaurants, sponsors, celebrities, and even more volunteers. The *New York Times* called it "The biggest idea of the year," and the *New Yorker* said it "reinvents charity for the 21st Century."

The Tap Project demonstrates how a subtle shift in an old message can exponentially increase new results. By making the donations more accessible (only a dollar, at a location you'll already be visiting), UNICEF makes lifesaving water more accessible.

There are many important messages out in the world. Most, almost all, will go ignored. It doesn't matter how valid and critical your message is if no one listens and responds.

We may not always like or enjoy messages that generate alarm. Often we don't. However, we do pay attention. Similarly, we may not always like or enjoy those we respect, but they earn our fascination. In our next trigger, prestige, we'll find out why.

Prestige

Why We Fixate on Symbols of Rank and Respect

At one point in history, a single tulip bulb was sold in exchange for four fat oxen, twelve fat sheep, four tons of butter, a thousand pounds of cheese, a complete bed, a suit of clothes, a silver cup, and large measures of rye, wheat, beer, and wine. The year was 1636, at the height of the Dutch hysteria for tulips. This hysteria became so extravagant, so delusional, so widespread, that modern economists pinpoint this as the world's first economic bubble.

Investors traded tulip bulbs in the stock exchanges, with prices depending not on beauty or perfume, but on scarcity and fashion. At the market's height, an investor offered twelve acres of prime land for one prestigious Viceroy bulb. Other varietals flaunted such cachet that they were given designer names corresponding to titles of exalted respect, such as "admiral" or "general."

The rarest tulips had spectacularly vivid petal colors. The most popular were Violetten, featuring purple or lilac infused on a white background, and Rosen, with red or pink against white. With designs such as flamboyant lines or flames against signature colors, these blossoms were more difficult to cultivate, but scarcity increased their price.

Today, as then, seeds grown from a flowering tulip bulb take between seven and twelve years to propagate. Cultivating the most desirable varieties of tulips requires years of investment, and the most valuable varieties grow the most slowly. Even after so many years of labor, these precious tulips bloom only in April and May for about a week. Therefore, the Dutch purchased actual tulip flowers for only two or three months out of the year. However, the real craze began in the afterseason. Owing to the frenzied demand, investors created a futures market in which traders signed purchase notaries to create a year-round market.

The tulip craze began to spread in a manner not unlike the tech bubble of 2000, or the real estate bubble of 2006. The French got wind of the outrageous profits, and joined in the speculation. Prices soared to such extraordinary heights that an entire network of values flipped on its head. So ferociously had the prestige trigger gripped the community of tulip buyers that they became obsessed with acquisition and value, competing with everyone else to acquire a flower worth more than the next investor's. Some investors reportedly paid upward of six times an annual salary, and in some cases more than the cost of a house, for a single flower bulb. A single flower could be worth more than the house in front of which it was planted.

The flowers themselves had no utility, of course. They couldn't be eaten, they had no medicinal use. Investors couldn't ride one to market, or pass it down as an heirloom. They couldn't even be carried in a wallet. Tulips were sold on the promise of prestige.

Then, as now, the most prestigious aspect of an asset could be the "idea" of it, and in this case, the "idea" of tulips was sold with the creation of the futures market. Feverish investors began selling off possessions and liquidating retirement accounts in order to buy . . . yep . . . tulips.

Yet what goes up must come down. In the case of tulip hysteria, the bust was fast and hard. As soon as the Dutch changed trading laws, allowing buyers to back out of tulip contracts for a small fee, the resulting market anxiety led to panic selling. Tulips may have been traded on an idea, but the collapse left many in real financial ruin.

Today, some historians debate to what degree tulip hysteria impacted the Dutch economy. Yet the importance of the story doesn't lie in being the first bubble of its kind, but in the fact that the principles surrounding value fluctuations and market dynamics often stem from fascination with prestige.

Your car loses value when you drive it off the lot, your DVD player is obsolete with the introduction of the next technology, and this season's must-haves become next season's has-beens. But that never stops the prestige trigger from gripping consumers and investors. It's in our nature to prove worth and value. People today are still drawn to objects and endeavors that represent social standing, and probably always will be. We'll be fascinated by prestige as long as we remain hardwired to compare ourselves to those around us.

What Is Prestige?

Fancy logos, designer brands, and famous European hotels might come to mind. But that's merely the obvious side of prestige. This trigger reveals a group's values and beliefs by identifying the pecking order among its members. Prestige rates people and objects relative to one another.

This trigger applies to any form of social position that demonstrates one member's position relative to others. By examining the basis upon which a group evaluates prestige, we can get a sense of that group's values and beliefs. Is the pecking order based upon education? Beauty? Social achievements? Specialty in a professional area? Number of appearances on *Letterman*? The ability to score tickets to a sold-out Miley Cyrus concert? Examining how a culture or company stacks up its members reveals its priorities.

Prestigious people can evoke admiration, but more often, competition and envy. Among corporate circles, fascination might be triggered by a framed Princeton diploma or an invitation to speak at the TED conference. In a second-grade classroom, the same status might mean winning a round of Spore video game. Both represent achievement, and carry implied "value" to the group.

As we saw with tulip hysteria, when the prestige trigger gains momentum, it creates irrational behavior. People go to great lengths to attain the object of their fascination. How can you make people fascinated to attain *you*? No matter what your personality or product, prestige can increase your perceived value. There are four ways: Develop emblems, set new standards, limit availability, and earn it. To begin, let's find out how emblems work.

Develop Emblems

Long before Dior and Gucci, societies were fascinated by prestige. In ancient times, coveted badges included coats of arms, specific colors, mode of wearing hair, wreaths, shoes, lineage, burial practices, certain seats, and insignia of office. In certain African tribes, where bravery and valor are more prestigious than commercial assets, scars are status symbols. In Western societies, a fat, pale body indicated wealth and success because only outdoor manual laborers were tanned and thin; today, a tanned, thin body is a status symbol more associated with a spinning class than spinning a combine harvester.

Just as they paid absurd prices for tulips 375 years ago, today people pay absurd prices for logos. Prestige emblems can cost a few billion dollars (a private island on The Palms), or a few cents (a nifty new stamp), but usually have little or no intrinsic value. Regardless of price tag or economy, these principles remain the same. Emblems themselves will change over time, but the fascination with emblems will not.

Emblems fulfill a deep, instinctive need because they say something *about us*. Abraham Maslow calls this "esteem": the need to feel important, respected, and recognized as an achiever. We satisfy this need by communicating our value to the world around us. A Mercedes Maybach, perhaps? Sure, yeah, it's expensive, but the price tag also comes with intangible extras like getting to consult with designers, craftsmen, and engineers. As a brand, the car is less of a "car," and more a statement of membership in an elite.

What to do if everyone in your social circle already has a Maybach? How, then, can a mogul make a statement? During the Japanese real estate boom an industrialist named Ryoei Saito showed just how creative the monied can get. Twice he paid world record prices for artwork, for a Van Gogh and a Renoir, and then he announced he planned to be buried with his paintings.*

---

* For that investment, one can only hope he's the most fascinating guy at the afterlife party.

Blue Bake-Off Ribbons and Pink Mary Kay Cadillacs

Emblems can be simple or elaborate, expensive or humble, but all share some degree of unattainability. Emblems incentivize people to stay a step ahead of everyone else. Bake-off champions show off blue ribbons. Mary Kay's top employees drive pink Cadillacs. Children collect autographs from Mickey and Minnie at Disney. Girl Scouts wear merit badges on uniforms. Proud fathers of newborns have hospital bands. Alcoholics Anonymous members mark sobriety with coins. Scholars frame Phi Beta Kappa keys.

By developing symbols of value, groups can strengthen participation and commitment. People eagerly work to acquire and show off emblems. So it only makes sense that companies should develop emblems of value.

Prestigious groups monitor access to remain sought-after, rare, and valuable. Insider brands usually control how many people get access to the brand; otherwise, oversaturation cheapens status and destroys value. Otherwise, subculture brands head directly to the strip mall. In 2004, the Ed Hardy tattoo-inspired brand launched onto the edgy glam-rock scene with its iconic skulls, tigers, and red rose designs, often combined with a "Love kills slowly" banner of hand-etched type. For this trend, once coveted by insiders, love doesn't kill slowly; it needs only five years. By 2009, line extension included (get ready): Ed Hardy–branded drinking water, candy, vodka and wine, coffee beans, disposable dinnerware, Koozies, Band-Aids, air fresheners, hand sanitizers, Smart Cars, hookahs, as well as a skull-adorned collection of diapers, sippy cups, and pacifiers.*

---

* At the time of this writing, the Ed Hardy by Christian Audigier line of bedding (including duvet cover and neck roll) was discounted 40 percent by at Macy's. Counterculture, meet outlet mall.

As exposure goes up, so do profits, but mystique among the original insider fans drops.

To establish fresh prestige, consider the existing standards—and how to set a new one.

Set a New Standard

Setting a new standard doesn't just change perceptions of a company; it shifts its entire category. Once set apart, a prestigious brand will have no alternatives, merely inferior substitutes.

When Grey Goose vodka was introduced, it threw down the ultraluxury vodka gauntlet. The price tag, literally double the cost of other vodkas on the shelf, was unthinkably high. Yet more incredibly, the price was established before the bottle was designed, before the distillery was named, and even before the vodka recipe itself was invented.

That might seem like putting the "cart before the goose," but not only did Grey Goose define a new "ultrapremium" vodka category, but within eight years, it closed the largest ever single brand sale when Bacardi bought the spirit for $2 billion. Instead of dogfighting with others to gain prestige, it simply forced an entire category to realign.

What about a brand? What if it falls behind its peer group? Once lost, prestige is difficult to reclaim. But as we'll see, not impossible.

What Happens When the World's Most Dazzling Diamonds Lose Their Sparkle?

No royalty, dynasty, or government empire can surpass the House of Winston in its legacy of celebrated jewels. The brand's glorious past includes many of the most famous diamonds, and diamond wearers, in history. As one fine example, the grande dame of gemstones, the Hope Diamond, began its dramatic history with Louis XIV. After peering down from its golden perch atop the crown jewels of France, it then spent time in the jewel boxes of Marie Antoinette and Countess du Barry before becoming the possession of Harry Winston. Winston donated the forty-five carats of dark blue perfection to the Smithsonian, where it now sits cushioned on display as specimen 2177868.* Diamonds from the Winston vault have commemorated some of the most renowned romances ever, from European royalty to Hollywood royalty. It was at Harry Winston that Richard Burton bought Elizabeth Taylor's engagement ring, and that Aristotle Onassis bought Jackie O's marquise. Marilyn Monroe gushed, "Talk to me, Harry Winston, talk to me!" in her classic 1953 rendition of "Diamonds Are a Girl's Best Friend." And not without reason. The House of Winston was known for selecting only the rarest gems, with only 0.01 percent of the world's reserves deemed worthy to sell under its name. Yet what makes the Winston brand even more precious are the stories behind the stones themselves.

---

* According to legend, the stone carried a grisly curse to all who owned it. As the story goes, the Hope Diamond originated as one of two glittering eyes on a statue of the goddess Sita, deep within a Hindu temple. After it was stolen, enraged temple priests swore that every owner would face a terrible fate. And indeed, subsequent owners met with rather unhappy endings: they were dethroned and beheaded, stabbed and starved, drowned in a shipwreck. Even jewelers trading the Hope were not immune; some succumbed to insanity, others to suicide. By 1908, the *Washington Post* published an article titled, "Hope Diamond Has Brought Trouble to All Who Have Owned It." All this mystique only increased the stone's fascination (not to mention its market value). In 1911, Pierre Cartier (of Cartier jewelers) enticed socialite Evalyn Walsh McLean to purchase the stone by embellishing the lurid tales of tragedy. McLean never fell prey to the curse, but instead, strapped the Hope Diamond to her dog's collar for walks, and frequently misplaced it at parties.

Mr. Winston once purchased a 726-carat stone in London, setting off a heated debate about the safest way to get it back to the States. A league of bodyguards? Chartered ship? Colossal insurance policy? Harry Winston wouldn't say which method he'd picked. Two weeks later, the priceless jewel arrived at his Fifth Avenue store, sent via standard registered mail, for 64 cents postage.

Shipping methods weren't Harry Winston's only nerve-racking decision. He cut many of his diamonds himself, often with tens of millions of dollars resting on a single mallet tap. Winston was dissatisfied with anything but flawlessness. Upon purchasing the famed 143-carat Star of Sierra Leone, he announced he would cleave away the ever-so-slightly flawed imperfections, thus greatly reducing the size of the stone. It was an extraordinarily risky maneuver, one that unleashed an outcry from diamond connoisseurs before he made the decision. But Winston picked up his tool, and struck the magnificent gem.

The resulting stone was only a fifth the size—but because it was flawless, it far surpassed the value of the original.

Later in his career, after negotiating the largest ever individual parcel sale of diamonds in history, Mr. Winston made one final request at the sale: "How about a little something to sweeten the deal?" His counterpart wordlessly took a 181-carat rough from his pocket, and rolled it across the table. The resulting D-flawless emerald-cut diamond has since been known as "The Deal Sweetener."

Considering Harry Winston's focus on detail, it's not difficult to understand that a little black box with the initials "HW" on the top was prestigiously fascinating. Yet after the passing of Mr. Winston himself, the House of Winston couldn't rely on the same old cues.

"Old New York" Starts to Seem . . . Well, Old

The House of Winston's Fifth Avenue flagship location dripped "old New York" cachet. Most of the hallowed diamonds were hidden away in a vault until requested, and patrons had to pass through a security gate to enter. The gray silk decor was described as "the inside of a coffin."

Overall, the setting boasted exclusivity and discretion to older shoppers, but for others, it was fussy and outdated. Putting the nail in the gray-satin-lined coffin, oversized "diamonds" rapidly became commonplace with the abundance of cubic zirconias. Five-carat earrings became rather humdrum.

Could the House of Winston reclaim prestige? As part of the Point One Percent* team charged with reestablishing the brand, we focused on the experience of prestige itself. Prestige is about rank. Just as Grey Goose established a new standard, so did the House of Winston need to claim an uppermost position. How?

While diamonds might be billions of years old, as with every product, their cultural context changes over time. To survive new competitors and a changing economy, every brand must adjust its fascination cues to survive. To trigger a higher level of prestige, we wooed the world's most legendary portrait photographer, Richard Avedon, to shoot movie stars such as Anjelica Huston and Mena Suvari wearing the mighty jewelry.

Next in the process, because I was the writer for the advertising, it was my turn to capture all this prestige in words. It wasn't easy. How to express just how good these diamonds

---

* What does the name Point One Percent mean? This agency only targets the 0.1 percent wealthiest consumers in the world. The agency was founded by Alexander Duckworth. (Imagine how much fun we had introducing ourselves in meetings together: Duckworth and Hogshead.)

actually are? And in just a few words, no less? A woman might own a Harry Winston necklace for years and still be lucky to encounter only ten people who could fully appreciate it.

To understand this experience for myself, I visited the flagship store. There in the vault, I tried on some of the world's most iconic pieces of jewelry. A forty-carat ring once owned by Jackie O. A $10 million necklace worn by an actress as she accepted her Academy Award. Pieces that are loaned only to A-level stars and brides in Dubai. Adorned with those weighty gems, I found out that there's a thrill in wearing the Earth's most precious offerings. At that point, the headlines almost wrote themselves:

People will stare.
Make it worth their while.
RSVP your regrets to the ordinary.
Watch the women watching the men watching you.

In 1867, Karl Marx had commented in *Das Kapital*, "If we could succeed, at a small expenditure of labour, in converting carbon into diamonds, their value might fall below that of bricks." Quite fortunately, the House of Winston proved him wrong, and their diamonds retained prestige. Any product can prove Marx wrong, and avoid commoditization, as long as it triggers fascination.

What might a nonluxury company learn from a purveyor of fine gemstones? People inherently compete within their peer group. Every product has the potential to become a prestige emblem. If that emblem sets a new standard, people work harder to achieve it. The value of that emblem isn't about the utility, so the cost of the item itself often doesn't matter, but rather, the signal of achievement it sends to *others*. As emblems go, a Winston necklace might come at a dear price; however, many emblems cost little in terms of actual market value.

Within your company, in the office, the same principle applies. If a manager can create an environment in which people compare themselves to one another, they often naturally seek to achieve just slightly more than those around them.

Grey Goose and Harry Winston set new standards. Now we'll look at prestige of a different sort: scarcity.

Limit Availability

Someone paid $14.3 million for a license plate.

No, the plate isn't made of solid gold, and it doesn't contain plutonium rocket fuel. It features the number 1. In the oil-rich and car-obsessed culture of Dubai, license plates are a matter of personal pride. Most plates have five digits. But the lower the number, the higher the price tag.

Increasing Price to Decrease Accessibility

Luxury brands offer the most blatant example of the desire for exclusivity. These brands trade on a very simple premise: A higher price tag isn't a barrier to purchase, but rather an incentive. Reports the *New York Times*, "In some cases, manufacturers adjust prices upward to make sure that their goods hang in good company, displayed alongside prestigious luxury brands."

Limiting availability isn't just confined to the Persian Gulf emirates and Fred Segal boutiques. In many cities, prestige can be described in five digits: the zip code.

You probably know 90210. But you might not know 31561, or 11771. These zip codes have become brand names to those in the know, communicating volumes of prestige in just five digits. The *New York Times* and CNN have both described a growing fascination with zip codes. Realtors report that increasingly, new residents "shop" for these numeric brands more fervently than the house itself. In Long Island the post office has received a flood of requests for neighborhoods to be annexed into more demographically desirable zip codes. Some residents even petition to change the zip code of their current area to increase their social standing. "Rather than admit to being status seekers, people generally claim that they are changing their zip code so that the Fire Department can locate them more readily in an emergency or to insure that their mail will get through or to allow their children to share their classmates' zip code. More often than not, however, the unspoken reason is upward mobility."

New York's billionaire mayor, Mike Bloomberg, referred to his city as a "high-end product," a description made more colorful by the *Wall Street Journal*: "Gucci on a metropolitan scale." Apparently, keeping up with the Joneses today might require moving next door to them.

Living Up to the Hype

Forcing others to wait (whether for an appointment, or a new product release) can raise prestige. However, limiting availability only works when people get something worthwhile in exchange. Every detail must justify the heightened cost.

Exercising Restraint

Limiting availability requires exercising some degree of restraint. In a culture obsessed with larger portions, mass production, and a store's cubic footage, prestigious people and companies know when to decline the super-sized in favor of a single mouthful of perfection. Quality, not quantity. Repeat after me: No thank you, Sam Walton.

While a snazzy zip code might certainly impress many people on the return address of a letter, in many instances, prestige is more about actions than purchases. Like respect, some of the most desirable status symbols must be earned.

Earn It

Economies change, and with them, tastes. In a recession, for instance, a FICO score over 800 can be more highly regarded than a 4,000-square-foot house. Debt-free liquidity earns more admiration than a bejeweled chihuahua peeking from a Hermès bag. A full-time job with benefits becomes more admired than a blinged-out car. The classic black Armani power suit can be pushed aside in the closet for the understated shirt and slacks.* For many, frugality is the new fashion.

During a financially stressful environment, people and companies use prestige to fascinate in new ways. When budgets tighten during a cutback or recession, the alarm trigger enters the picture and prestige cues can shift dramatically. Diversifying prestige cues beyond mere name recognition helps prestige-oriented brands avoid taking a hit when people no longer want overt displays. Prestige demands meaning in order to justify the fascination.

The Path to Prestige Is Slick with Sweat Equity

Few of us will enjoy the advantages of Kennedy lineage or Swiss bank accounts. But don't give up yet. Increasingly, prestige

---

* A note on prestige: The word "classy" isn't when it's spelled with a *k*. Trust me on this one.

lives in our accomplishments, network, and personal reputation (elements more within our control than being a royal firstborn). Modern prestige comes from running a marathon, winning a Rhodes scholarship, or in some cases, even procuring a limited-edition Prius.

For one form of prestige, people invest a minimum of 39.5 years, with a high probability of at least as many broken or dislocated fingers and toes. In exchange, they get a piece of fabric. A black one. Tang See Do, an American-style version of the Korean martial arts, rarely awards its eighth-level black belt. As with other levels of black belts, this status has nothing to do with age, economic status, or social status. In the classroom, a green-belted CEO might bow to his black-belted assistant.

Like our next trigger, power, the most authentic and lasting fascinations require you to earn them.

Power

Why We Focus on the People and Things That Control Us

Olympic athlete Dominique Moceanu was not just *any* gymnast. She was a fourteen-year-old member of the U.S. Olympic Gymnastics team, a darling of the 1996 Atlanta games, achieving the stratospheric heights of gymnastic success. And hers was not just any Olympic team: It was the beloved "Magnificent Seven" that won gold for the USA. Moceanu and her team only added to an already unprecedented track record earned by her coaches, Bela and Martha Karolyi. The Karolyis also coached Mary Lou Retton, Nadia Comaneci, and thirteen other world champions.

Yet Moceanu believes her Olympic gold medal cost too much. In July 2008, Moceanu criticized Bela and Martha Karolyi, and called for Martha's removal from Olympic training (Bela had since retired). Moceanu cites "mental and physical abuse," including strict demands, lack of compassion, and dietary restrictions.*

Under the influence of the power trigger, people submit

---

* Dominique's name comes from *dom*, the Latin root meaning "master" or "lord," the same root as "dominate."

to being controlled. Most forms of training work this way: A student relinquishes some degree of power to a teacher, in exchange for greater achievement. But sometimes, great rewards come at great cost. Where does training stop, and abuse of power begin? Or as the *New York Times* headline asks of Moceanu's charges, "How much is too much?"

Dominique trained with different coaches to attempt a comeback in 2006. However, USA Gymnastics rejected her from competing at nationals because "Moceanu wasn't physically prepared to compete."

What Is "Power"?

No matter where you rank on the pecking order, no matter your age or gender, no matter your continent or political view, power fascinates you. It's a response as involuntary as it is primal.

As the alphas of the pack, powerful people control our behavior in a myriad of ways. Wordlessly, they set the rules. Who's powerful? CEOs and prime ministers. Black belts and Boy Scout leaders. Terrorists. Oil sheiks, film critics, and teacher's pets. Firstborns, matriarchs, and Big Brother. Though their leadership differs, powerful people share an ability to both *make* decisions and *influence* decisions.

Anything can trigger power, if it controls its environment. Drug cartels use power. Objects and events can trigger power by controlling their environment: raging hurricanes, killer whales, and Greek gods of mythology. Even the lowly red stop sign uses power, by invoking the law.

In his book *Superclass*, David J. Rothkopf describes why:

> Power is, of course, hard to quantify. Wealth is often a source of power. Position regularly translates into

power. Perhaps the most ancient source of power is grounded in subtler things, like access or ideas. There is no single or universally accepted metric for power, so a certain amount of subjective judgment is inevitable. Determining who has it and who does not is made more difficult because some of the most influential among us commonly mask their power or use it infrequently.

In positive circumstances, power can motivate others to rise to their best. Used differently, it can unjustly intimidate or persecute. Gandhi persuaded differently from Genghis Khan, yet both commanded the multitudes with political mastery.

The Spectrum of Power

All seven triggers live on a spectrum. In the case of power, it ranges from delicate suggestion to crushing force. A meter maid uses a slight form of power, whereas a hijacker on a plane uses the same trigger to its maximum extent.

Under the influence of extreme power, individuals have little choice. Their behavior is controlled by someone (or something) else. People obey because they must, as a matter of survival. Classic example: the iron-fisted hand of a communist regime. You'll work hard, and you'll like it!

Yet lest you think power is all hammer and sickle, take a look at this trigger's flip side. Power isn't necessarily over-powering. It can guide gently, even lovingly. It's a necessary ingredient in many forms of structure, training, and motivation to achieve higher results. A parent uses power with an infant by shaping sleep patterns, feeding times, and language development. A parent might also use this trigger with a high school student through a weekly allowance or use of the family car. Either way, the goal is not to defeat the child, but to make her stronger.

Whether parental or dictatorial, authority figures use power to control us. This trigger weaves itself throughout our life every day, guiding our behavior. When our manager sends a seemingly casual text message on Friday afternoon mentioning a report that's now needed for Monday morning, our personal weekend plans just got wrecked. But we're "persuaded" to skip the cookout and head into the office on Saturday because we're fascinated by the prospect of a promotion. (In addition to power, the threat of unemployment triggers alarm.)

Used intelligently and selectively, this trigger strengthens your reputation and earns respect. In a competitive marketplace, it can give a decided upper hand. Power offers three paths: dominate, control the environment, and, finally, reward and punish. Let's begin with domination.*

Dominate

In the presence of power, we instinctively become submissive. When we're in the presence of someone who is more powerful, our innate response mechanisms are altered—translating into essentially a "deer in headlights" response, because "your body is preparing to have heightened attentiveness to what others are doing and how you're being evaluated," says Deborah Gruenfeld of the Stanford Graduate School of Business. We know, for example, that there are actually distinct differences in serotonin levels based on position in the hierarchy—and that serotonin levels change as animal subjects move into alpha or beta position.

---

* Because I'm the author and I say so. That's why.

When we are talking to a more powerful person, experts report, our personal boundaries can lower, making us resistant or skeptical. Our body language and speech patterns usually become deferential. We're more open to suggestion, more easily persuaded, and more likely to be dominated.

We all willingly allow ourselves to take a backseat in certain situations. But some people go to a greater extreme. They eagerly pay to be dominated. Even humiliated. (No, not by a dominatrix with a leather whip . . . by a chef with a very sharp knife.)

The Sushi Dictators

You may remember the Soup Nazi from *Seinfeld*. But are you familiar with the Sushi Dictators? These guys aren't paid actors, and the clientele is real. Each dictator has his own irritable quirks, but in many cases, patrons aren't allowed to order because the chef selects your meal. If you look up Sushi Nozawa in LA, it's one of the highest-rated restaurants in terms of the food. The *Zagat* description, however, clearly calls out its infamous reputation: "Makes the Soup Nazi look polite." *Wall Street Journal* reporter Katy McLaughlin describes this *omakase* tradition, which means "trust the chef," and explains that some consumers go because they think they're getting an authentic meal. But as psychologist David Stewart explains in the article, "people value praise more when it comes from people who don't give it out easily." People go to these restaurants in search of both "modest risk" and "approbation," Stewart says, "perhaps in the form of an uni handroll."

When I lived in LA, one of my favorite restaurants was Sushi Sasabune. More a fluorescent-lit, dingy greasy spoon than a sushi mecca, it had yellowed handwritten signs on the walls that said threateningly, "No California roll. No bowl of rice." (These are often favorites of the budget-conscious, or of sushi newbies, who tend to prefer tamer Americanized sushi.) Instead of name tags, every waiter's shirt simply said, "Trust me." This was an order, not a request. Chefs occasionally yell at customers for making a poor choice, and kick out a certain number of patrons each month to keep it interesting. This power play wouldn't work if the food couldn't live up to the hype, but this sushi is so fresh it almost bites back.

Can you persuade others to obey you? Yes, you can. And if you use domination as keenly as the Sushi Dictators, you'll even be tipped extra for it.

Provoking Inferiority Complexes

Who said fascinating people always play nice? Not in this trigger they don't. The Sushi Dictators emphasize insecurities. Aggressive negotiators prey upon weakness. Be polite, if you please. But if you're ready to dial up your power, you might need to take off the gloves, even if they're white kid gloves.

Marketers kindle insecurities all the time, and with great effectiveness. You might say that insecurities pay an ad agency's salaries. After all, if consumers aren't concerned about a problem, they won't buy a product to solve it. Bad breath and body odor weren't always offenses punishable by social ostracism—not until advertisers needed to sell more mouthwash and deodorant. Dry Idea commanded us, "Never let them see you sweat." Sure antiperspirant told us, "Raise your hand if you're sure," and showed us how icky it was to be *un*-sure. Yellowish tooth aren't exactly beauty assets, but they weren't stigmas until teeth whiteners showed how embarrassed we should be without flashcube-white teeth.

The alarm trigger shows that negative *consequences* prompt

action. This principle applies here as well. Consumers buy products to solve problems; the more negative and immediate the consequences, the greater a consumer's fascination with purchase. By provoking insecurities around our parenting skills, sexual prowess, intellect, and financial savvy, products trigger fascination.

Taking the Alpha Stance

Ranking systems fascinate us because they establish the group's "celebrities," or alpha members. Many groups invoke power by establishing a clear ranking system. It's even apparent in high school cliques: Without much effort, cliques form unspoken rules about who's in charge. Social networking sites do this all the time, listing each user's number of followers, offering easy public tools to rank a user's influence within the network.

What if there's conflict within a group about which member is the alpha leader? Who has the most power: the greatest ability to control and influence the environment? That's where things get tricky. Start a staring contest with a growling pit bull, for instance, and the dog won't be the one to flinch first.* Someone who *is* able to stare down a pit bull: Cesar Millan, expert dog trainer, aka the "Dog Whisperer." Yet expertise is only one half of his power. Equally if not more important is the execution of his experience: A combination of knowledge and tough love amplifies his domination.

Celebrity Monkey Paparazzi

The next time you're in the grocery store checkout line and find yourself staring at a charismatic athlete, billionaire mogul, or

---

* There's a reason why that "dog bites man" isn't a fascinating hook.

world-famous movie star's face on a magazine cover, blame your DNA. Just as we're instinctively fascinated by faces, we stare at the power. No matter where we rank on the social food chain, leaders fascinate us. Our obsession with powerful people is far older than *People* magazine. We inherited it from our hairier ancestors.

Deep within our tribal psyche, we share a need to focus on the most powerful members of our group. It's a raw, primal catalyst. Programmed into our social code is a need to "follow the leader," to find role models and fixate upon them. Duke University neurobiologist Dr. Michael Platt affirmed this by developing a scientific experiment that I'll call "*Entertainment Weekly* Goes to the Lab."

Platt offered thirsty rhesus monkeys a choice: a drink of their favorite beverage, or an opportunity to look at photos of "celebrity" monkeys (the Jay-Z and Beyoncé of the monkey kingdom). Celebrity monkeys were those that commanded attention in their pack, through power, food, and sexual magnetism. Not only did the monkeys want to look at their celebrities, but so strong was the fascination with power that the monkeys chose photo viewing over drinking. And even the celebrity monkeys were fascinated by images of fellow celeb monkeys.

Control the Environment

Every day, we allow others to control our personal environment. We agree to iTunes' terms of use, or take off our shoes for TSA security at the airport. On Facebook, users operate within a highly regimented interface that's quite different from MySpace's zany options (and which one is winning the social media wars?). iTunes, TSA, and Facebook all use power to control their environments, and control us in those environments.

What happens if an entire organization increases power to improve results? As we saw with gold medalist Dominique Moceanu, power can push performance—but not without price. In the words of the *New York Times*: How much is too much?

Meet Landmark Education, a "personal training and development company."

The Most Fascinating Organization in the World?

In Part I, we learned the six Gold Hallmarks of a Fascinating Message:

- Provokes strong and immediate emotional reactions
- Creates advocates
- Becomes "cultural shorthand" for a specific set of actions or values
- Incites conversation
- Forces competitors to realign around it
- Triggers social revolutions

With these criteria, Landmark Education Corporation is surely among the world's most fascinating companies. Most people have never heard of this insular organization, but once introduced, they're unlikely to forget it. Landmark persuades a high percentage of its attendees to make significant changes in their lives, yet simultaneously provokes and polarizes them. It accumulates fanatics, even evangelists, as well as heated debate from detractors. Within the self-help or personal development industry, it's a reference point around which others define themselves. Yet while not everyone agrees with Landmark's methods, if you can learn their secrets, your message can become more fascinating, too.* Landmark describes itself as a "global educational enterprise committed to the fundamental principle that people have the possibility of success, fulfillment, and greatness." Said more plainly, Landmark teaches self-help courses. More than a million people have completed Landmark's introductory program, the Forum, in twenty-one countries. Surprisingly little is known about the techniques used in Landmark's coursework. The privately held organization releases little data, and attendees sign a six-page non-disclosure agreement.† It's difficult to unveil much about Landmark, especially its methodology (which, as we know, increases mystique). Most information comes from anecdotal stories and input from previous participants.

Here are two things that *are* known. And while these facts seem to contradict each other, they both stem from the unique way in which Landmark controls its environment.

- *First, Landmark achieves extraordinary results.*
  The majority of participants describe the Landmark

---

* A Harvard Business School case study titled "Landmark Education Corporation: Selling a Paradigm Shift," describes coursework that is "intended to provide individuals and organizations with an insight into how to become more effective and/or access to a way of being which they had not thought possible."

† The NDA includes multiple variations on the following language: "a very small number of people who have no personal or family history of mental illness or drug abuse have reported experiencing brief, temporary episodes of emotional upset ranging from heightened activity, irregular or diminished sleep, to mild psychotic-like behavior . . . to psychosis occasionally requiring medical care and hospitalization." The release also mentions suicide. The *Washington Post* reports on one former participant's lawsuit: "Three days after attending the Forum, according to testimony, Ney suffered a breakdown and was committed to a psychiatric institute in Montgomery County. She was held there for two weeks, at times heavily drugged and strapped to a bed to prevent her from harming herself."

Forum as a life-changing program. In a Yankelovich
study, 90 percent of participants reported that their Landmark Forum experience "exceeded their expectations." An
IMC, Inc., study reported that 94 percent of graduates
said it made "a profound, lasting difference in the way
they live their lives," and 93 percent said that it was "one
of the most effective programs" they'd taken.

*   *Second, Landmark is controversial.*
    The organization is often compared to Scientology, and
    accused of using cultlike methods. (As we saw in Part I,
    cults achieve the very highest levels of fascination among
    followers.) An expert likened Landmark's methods to "the
    process used by the Soviets in preparing confessions for
    their show trials or the first stage of the brainwashing
    process." The program is illegal in France.

Just how does Landmark achieve such remarkably high approval ratings? And why all the fuss?

Landmark wields the power trigger in unique ways. While
"controlling the environment" might sound like an elaborate
show to stage, this company does so by directing basic elements of surroundings and process, proving that even subtle
changes can make a message dramatically more fascinating.

What's the point of all this protocol? Why does Landmark
go to such great lengths to enforce its own power? Psychologists
suggest that when people are no longer in charge of basic elements of a situation (such as where they sit, or when they go to the
restroom), they must give over some degree of control that they
normally use to define their independence, and thus themselves.
Many researchers have proven that once people have agreed to

let go of small details, they become more willing to submit to the more significant changes. By gradually releasing self-control, they open themselves up to more significant changes, and to the leader. The leader's message sinks in far more deeply, "destabilizing" an individual, and shedding his natural resistance.

This destabilization, according to experts, makes people more open to new interpretations. It's how brainwashing works, how boot camp works, and to a greater or lesser degree, it's how most immersive learning works. Often, immersive learning begins small, with seemingly insignificant details of environment.* One sociologist describes how a "structured" and "organized" seminar format increases "total power" for the leader. The more specific a leader's direction, the greater his potential influence. Within every type of interaction—an interview, a negotiation, a confrontation—hundreds of variables shape the result, and the more variables we can govern around a message, the more we control the environment. By convincing the audience to follow specific rules, leaders can make their message become more fascinating.†

Applying Landmark's Methods to Your Next Meeting

Praise or condemn Landmark's techniques, but like Bela and Martha Karolyi, this organization very effectively uses power to achieve remarkable results. How might this apply in our own lives?

---

* In the early nineties, I took a few Landmark courses, and saw firsthand how effectively they utilize subtle power. The program allowed us to eat or use the restroom only on a strict schedule, the room's layout adhered to a rigid seating arrangement, the decor was austere, body language was monitored, exercises were mandatory, fifteen-hour days were nonnegotiable, and bathroom breaks were infrequent. Other participants noticed what seemed to be intentional light and temperature fluctuations.

† Please note: Exercising power doesn't make you a great leader, it merely demonstrates your ability to regulate. You will be defined, and ultimately judged, on the quality and effectiveness of your message.

For instance, we might want "total power" during a presentation, to make sure our message persuaded and captivated the audience. What general themes from Landmark could we adapt and apply?

We'd begin exerting power in a meeting before the meeting ever began, crafting the interaction so it unfolds on our terms rather than on someone else's, by accident. We'd consider every aspect of how an audience experiences a presentation: the layout of the room, the schedule, even the refreshments. We'd eliminate distractions, such as exterior noise or interruptions, so our message has less competition. We'd increase mystique by selectively choosing which pieces of information to reveal. We'd monitor the physical experience of the meeting, including even the comfort level of the chairs (or in the case of Landmark, their discomfort). To ratchet up control even further, we wouldn't ask participants just to turn off phones, but to surrender them for the duration of the program.

Rarely do we seek to be manipulative or dictatorial. But we do want to persuade. A fascinating meeting clearly positions a leader, and allows an audience to immerse itself in the message. Begin that process from the very first impression.

Head & Shoulders Had It Right

Remember the tagline "You never get a second chance to make a first impression"? Maître d's know this, telling us when and where we'll be going. Nightclub bouncers don't get chatty about their decision-making process for who gains access to the Cristal-drenched VIP room.*

You already know that a strong first impression begins with

---

* Plus they wear black double-breasted suits, which may or may not be your idea of a fashion statement, but it ups the intimidation factor.

confident body language and eye contact, and a firm handshake. Yet this approach doesn't apply just to in-person meetings. The same is also true when introducing any type of message, from a disciplinary warning to a routine internal memo. Carefully manage your message and reinforce it. Minimizing errors becomes even more essential when power is your trigger. Mistakes, such as website glitches or incomplete data, deflate your position. Nobody wants to watch how sausage is made.

Whether subtle or overt, this style of interaction increases domination. This domination exerts some degree of pressure on others, making them less likely to reject a message.

Reward and Punish

Dominique Moceanu's success with the Karolyis, and her subsequent approbation of them, demonstrates the great influence of reward and punishment. When people covet a reward, even a small one, they become fascinated by the prospect of attaining it. If they begin to believe that the reward is worth a potential downside, they'll go to great lengths to achieve it. In many cases, unreasonable lengths.*

---

* I admit it, I jump through hoops for frequent flier rewards—my speaking schedule demands last-minute flight availability, and, okay, maybe I also do it because of the perks. Yet one year I was sixteen thousand miles shy of maintaining my premier membership with Delta. I calculated that I could accumulate just that many miles by flying from Jacksonville to Seattle . . . twice. So off to Seattle I flew, back and forth, twice, without ever leaving the airport. But, it turns out, I was still a few miles short (Delta, if you're listening, I'm still peeved). I discovered this on December 29, which meant I had only two days left to earn the miles. But at this point, I was so close I could almost feel the leather seats underneath me, so I flew to New York on New Year's Eve. The flight was delayed, which meant I could possibly lose the necessary miles for the calendar year. I told the flight attendant my tale of woe, and not only did I snag an extra bag of peanuts, but the pilots radioed the ground crew, who lined up and greeted me with an orange-flashlight escort to my waiting return flight. So anyway. Back to the ridiculous, idiotic behavior of people on a quest for reward.

When offering a reward, don't be afraid to put it well out of reach, enticing others to push outside their comfort zone to achieve it. But a warning: If negative reinforcement becomes too strict, or punishment too frequent, it sparks a backlash.

Rules and Consequences

Callers to Suze Orman's show already know that they risk her signature wrath by fessing up to their huge credit card debt. Suze has developed governing principles in her own metaphoric playbook, and the audience knows the consequences for breaking them. Whether you're establishing rules for a companywide policy on time sheets, or establishing a prom curfew for your teenager, don't get namby-pamby in enforcement.

Many leaders heighten the power trigger by withholding praise. They hand out compliments sparingly, even when rules are followed correctly, because praise gains affection but not necessarily respect. Yet not everyone withholds praise and support. Some gain power by boosting a sense of power in others. Viagra did this in the late nineties.*

The Big Power of the Little Blue Pill

Impotence is probably as old as sex itself. In *Medieval Masculinities*, Vern Bullough tells us that in the Middle Ages, the condition was "a threat not only to a man's maleness but to society. Potency came to be not only the way in which a male defined himself, but how he was defined by society." So great was the implied meaning that impotence could prevent or

---

* Curious to know pre-Viagra options, I turned to *Impotence*, by Angus McLaren, who reports that early aphrodisiacs included "windy, warm, and wet foods" as well as "the brains of male sparrows mixed with filberts and billy goat grease."

nullify marriage, and serve as grounds for divorce.* A man who couldn't trigger power was no man at all.

A generally dismal view of the condition continued into the twentieth century. But then, in 1998, Pfizer renamed "impotence" as "erectile dysfunction." Presto—unlike impotence, erectile dysfunction was a urological issue (merely a little plumbing glitch!), rather than a humiliating psychological neurosis. By changing the name of the condition, Pfizer and pitchman Bob Dole changed far more. No longer were anyone's personal inadequacies to blame. In its second year on the market, worldwide Viagra sales topped $1 billion in fascination-enhanced sales.

Next up, we'll meet vice: the bad girl of the fascination triggers. The one who stays out too late and drinks too much whisky, and convinces you to come along. Do join in, won't you?

---

* How to prove if a man was impotent? At one point the Church assigned "seven honest women" to the task of determining whether or not a man was impotent. At other times, members of the court were pressed into action, standing around the bed during copulation to confirm a man's performance (or performance anxiety).

Vice

Why We're Tempted by "Forbidden Fruit"

Smart organizations recognize a business opportunity when they see it. So when Prohibition began on January 17, 1920, the Mafia expanded beyond gambling and thievery, and into the far more profitable pursuit of bootlegging. Overnight, the manufacture, sale, and distribution of alcoholic beverages became illegal in the United States. As the black market for hard liquor flourished, the mob became wealthier than ever, growing so pervasive and powerful from alcohol profits that Chicago mob boss Al Capone earned more than $100 million a year.* The Mafia held a national convention in 1928 to formalize its reign, even discussing a nationwide crime syndicate.

The "Noble Experiment," as Prohibition was called, didn't dampen drinking. When drinking moved underground into

---

* Allow me to put this into economic perspective. In an article on the top-earning professional athletes, *Sports Illustrated* reports that Tiger Woods earns "the inconceivable total of $100 million." Capone's income, translated into 2008 dollars, is well over a billion dollars annually. Surprisingly, Capone was not paying personal income tax on these dollars. Eliot Ness indicted him in 1931.

speakeasy clubs, beating Prohibition became a hobby enjoyed by millions of Americans. Former proponent John D. Rockefeller admitted its failure, writing that "drinking has generally increased; the speakeasy has replaced the saloon; a vast army of lawbreakers has appeared; many of our best citizens have openly ignored Prohibition; respect for the law has been greatly lessened; and crime has increased to a level never seen before." Thanks to Prohibition, the vice trigger made Americans thirstier than ever.

To Capone's disappointment, Prohibition was repealed in 1933, greatly reducing the underworld's illegal profits. Americans found new forms of vice, and the mob found new business activities.*

What Is "Vice"?

The devil sitting on your shoulder, whispering in your ear? He's whispering vice. When we're told we *can't* have something, this trigger of fascination can take hold and make us want more.

Cultures have always recognized this phenomenon. Pandora had her box, Lot's wife's curiosity turned her into a pillar of salt, Romeo and Juliet loved more passionately (and died more passionately) because their parents tried to keep them apart. One bite of an apple got Adam and Eve booted out of paradise. And let's not forget the cat, whose curiosity proved her undoing.

Rules are not often fascinating, but bending them, very much so. When we're tempted to push a boundary, or deviate

---

* Don't feel too bad for Capone. The Mafia was able to console itself by increasing profits from prostitution, drugs, labor racketeering, and loan sharking.

from standard norms, we're in a vice grip. Vice includes everything you *want* to do, and know you *shouldn't* do, but still just *might* do.

Vice takes many forms in our daily lives, usually masquerading as guilty pleasures: vanity, insincerity, excessive spending, sexuality, and other qualities easily found inside every Victoria's Secret mall location.

The Push-Up Bra: A Wearable White Lie

We each indulge in a few transgressions. That third slice of pepperoni pizza, high blood pressure be damned. Sleeping in on Sunday when the grass needs mowing. Sneaking the occasional cigarette at a bar. Texting while driving, or reading trashy gossip magazines while getting a pedicure. It's watching *Nip/Tuck*, reading DailyCandy, or logging onto PerezHilton.com.

Not every type of vice fascinates every person, but we all have a few gleeful gratifications hidden in our behavior.* We all challenge virtue now and again. (If you've ever pressed the close button from inside the elevator doors while someone is rushing in, well, there you go.)

Please Use Responsibly

A little vice goes a long way, so customize your message by using it in combination with other triggers.

Few of us intend to deliberately lead someone into temptation. Yet unless we understand how we're influencing action, we could be doing just that, making this trigger unexpectedly important. We'll soon find out how a message that

---

* In the Kelton Survey, 60 percent of Americans said they would be willing to bend their morals, standards, or loyalties in order to have a more interesting life.

unintentionally triggers vice can accomplish an entirely different result than intended. People do the exact opposite of what they're told. Just ask the Prohibitionists.

The word "vice" comes from the Latin *vitium*, meaning "failing or defect," because vices reveal our weaknesses. These weaknesses don't necessarily force us into a morally bad place, and they're not always "wrong" or "evil." Rather, vice tempts us to break out of strict norms, or bend the rules a bit.

Ready to have a dance with the bad girl? A whit of vice can spice up any humdrum conversation or unremarkable brand. We have four pillars of vice at our disposal: Create taboos. Lead others astray. Define absolutes. And give a wink.

Forbidden fruit would not taste so juicy if it weren't forbidden. Let's start by exploring the juicy world of taboos.

Create Taboos

It's easy to spot how female celebrities flaunt taboos to trigger our fascination (though not necessarily our respect). Porn tapes from eye-candy stars such as Paris Hilton and Kim Kardashian increased their exposure. Reality stars fight for the "villain" role, including Omarosa from *The Apprentice* and Simon Cowell from *American Idol*, because villains earn notoriety. The patron saint of vice, Madonna, stokes the vice machine by humping the stage in a wedding dress, or dancing in lingerie next to burning crosses, or starring in hardcover erotica stashed behind the bookstore counter. Monica Lewinsky launched a handbag line with little more than a tête-à-tête with a cigar on her résumé.

The Profits of Controversy

Banned material isn't always wrapped in plain brown paper wrappers. It also comes in covers with titles that read *The*

Catcher in the Rye, or *American Heritage Dictionary*, or *Where's Waldo?** In 1882, the great American poem *Leaves of Grass* was banned for obscene content. Sales increased so dramatically from the publicity that poet Walt Whitman bought a house from the royalties.

Herein lies a key benefit of vice: Nobody yawns when vice seeps into the conversation. It never fails to get people talking (and talking and talking, and often, buying).

We're especially fascinated when our heroes fall from heights, into the fiery infernos of vice.

The Golden Swimmer Takes a Dive

Months after the Beijing Olympics, fourteen-time gold medalist swimmer Michael Phelps was photographed in 2009 smoking from a bong. (You have no idea whatsoever what a "bong" is, right? . . . Good, just checking. Me neither.) Experts predicted that the photo would cost him millions of dollars in endorsements. But no. Quite interestingly, the same trigger that fascinated Phelps in that infamous photo has also grabbed hold of lucrative sponsors as well.

The notorious photo, circulated around the globe, happens to display an Omega watch on Phelps's left wrist. A spokesman for Omega Watches crowed, "You can't buy this kind of product placement—believe me, we've tried! . . . He's modeling one of our blinged-out products as he expertly removes the carb from the bong, which we will also be selling replicas of: The

---

* It's difficult to identify exactly how the *Where's Waldo* series of children's books earned the distinction of being among the American Library Association's one hundred most challenged books between 1990 and 2000. Rumor has it that as a young readers search to find Waldo amid the intricately drawn cartoon images, they can also find topless sunbathers and other naughty bits. Get out your magnifying glasses, kids.

Poseidon, as we are proudly calling it, holds actual water, just like what Michael Phelps swims in!"

Phelps not only "expertly removes the carb from the bong," as the Omega spokesman announced, but he also knows how to tap the next pillar of vice: leading others astray.

Lead Others Astray

Las Vegas, the uncontested vice capital of the world, doesn't just lead others astray: It leads them directly into the den of iniquity.

When Las Vegas conspiratorially promises in your ear, "What happens here, stays here," your mind goes berserk with all the wicked possibilities. That tagline taps into an incredibly complex mind map of desires, fears, protocols, expectations, and even religious and moral codes. When you hear those words, you almost pause to consider exactly *what* it is that would stay in Vegas.

To compete in any crowded marketplace, you must lead someone astray from his usual behavior. If you're a restaurateur, you must tempt patrons to order more expensive bottles of wine and a dessert course. Every process of vice starts by getting someone to consider what he *could* have, and *desires* to have, but *doesn't* have. Yet.

Making Guilty Pleasures Guiltier

Sometimes, changing behavior starts with changing the channel. Have you seen the TV teen drama *Gossip Girl*? It's a popular guilty pleasure, but it wasn't always so popular. With initially modest ratings for this startup show, the network decided to do something bold to raise its profile.

Major news outlets skewered *Gossip Girl* for its depiction of bad behavior. The show didn't apologize for the storylines—it celebrated them. Advertising posters wallpapered all over major cities used the negativity to tempt viewers: "Very Bad for You," one poster screamed. "A Parent's Worst Nightmare," and "A Nasty Piece of Work," declared others. And perhaps most delightfully, "Mind-Blowingly Inappropriate."

Was it effective? Oh yes. Ratings increased substantially. Viewers celebrate the show that celebrates bad behavior.

Define Absolutes

Let's start with an experiment, shall we?

We're in a laboratory together, you and I. It's starkly white, without decoration or distraction of any kind. On the table in front of you, I place an unadorned black box. It has a lid, which is shut but unlocked. "You can look at this box," I say, "you can touch it. But you cannot open it." Then I leave the room, stopping only to add one final reminder, "Whatever you do, *do not open this box.*"

Some people would never consider opening the box. But chances are, as time passed alone in that white room, you might stare at the unlocked box and start to wonder, "What's inside, and why can't I open it? Must be pretty good to create all the fuss." If more time passed, you might begin questioning my warnings. After all, I haven't given you any meaningful reason to obey me. You don't even know me, or more importantly, trust me.

Now, imagine you can see through the windows of this white laboratory, into other rooms, each filled with people like you. They each have a black box in front of them, but there's a difference: They've each opened their boxes. And what glorious things must be inside! They seem ecstatic. These people start to notice you and your unopened box. They encourage you to open yours, despite my order. You're torn. You want to follow the orders, but a mix of rebellion and temptation now stirs you.

"What if," you might say to yourself, ". . . what if I just take a small peek?"

Just a small peek. That, my friend, is a gateway drug.

Why "Just Say No" Leads to "Just Say Maybe"

You've probably seen those red-and-black bumper stickers encouraging us to "DARE to keep your kids off drugs." The DARE program (Drug Abuse Resistance Education) has a strong premise and participation. Police officers teach kids about the dangers of drugs and violence by focusing curriculum on "refusal skills," or eight ways to "just say no." Theoretically, it works on many levels: Kids interact with police officers, police officers become more involved on a grassroots level with the school, and everyone learns how to refuse drugs. Spending billions of dollars, the DARE program has been deployed in 80 percent of school districts in the U.S. and in fifty-four other countries with a zero-tolerance policy.

There's just one problem. It doesn't work. New research shows that at best it prompts no change in behavior, and at worst, it *increases* affinity for drugs. Not only does DARE not keep kids off drugs, it makes them more likely to use drugs.

The respected program indoctrinates thirty-six million of our youth each year and costs the United States approximately $1.13 billion annually. Yet the U.S. Surgeon General, Department of Education, and the General Accounting Office have all labeled the program ineffective.

Rocky Anderson, former mayor of Salt Lake City, eliminated

his city's DARE program. Anderson announced his contempt in *Rolling Stone*: "I think your organization has been an absolute fraud on the people of this country. For you to continue taking precious drug-prevention dollars when we have such a serious and, in some instances, growing addiction problem is unconscionable." When my researcher spoke with Anderson, he was more adamant, calling the program "whoredom."

Why doesn't DARE work? And more important, what does? To answer these questions, my team and I did several weeks of primary and secondary research. After reading the findings and interviewing other anti-drug program leaders, we discovered specific ways in which the program unintentionally triggers vice in teens: DARE's zero-tolerance policy encourages kids not only to engage in an abstinence lifestyle, but also to turn in their friends, and even report parents' drug use; it dispenses fear-based information about drugs for shock effect and doesn't draw distinctions between substances (e.g., beer versus meth); and the authority figures (police officers) are not trusted and familiar people. The program heightens both mistrust and mystique.

In a nutshell: The research suggests not that prevention doesn't work, but that this particular model of prevention—while well intended—doesn't work. Like the unopened black box, it turns drugs into forbidden fruit.

The Teenage Brain, a Vice Magnet

All seven triggers affect decision making, whether or not we intend them to. Using vice, however, can cause the exact opposite effect rather than the one intended. Especially with teenagers. Vice, when combined with mistrust and mystique, increases the likelihood of engaging in behavior.

In the chapter on alarm, we saw Luke Sullivan's epiphany about drunk driving and teenagers: a graphic photo of a car wreck won't effectively dissuade teenage drivers. For teens, fear isn't necessarily a reason to avoid something. It can even heighten the attraction, in a natural, normal part of the brain's development through adolescence.* According to a recent study, seventeen-year-olds commit more crimes than any other age group. And in another study, college students age eighteen to twenty-four were more likely than their older counterparts to take risks across a broad spectrum of activities, from not wearing a bicycle helmet, to riding with a drunk driver, to experimenting with illegal drugs.[†]

Unintentionally Triggering Vice

Rules and policies are an important part of a functioning workplace, but can backfire when employees feel micromanaged, or don't understand the reasoning behind them. Ever see *Office Space*? The proverbial TPS report makes employees want to disobey, if only for the thrill of rebellion.

The same applies to any authority figure. Parents can trigger defiance by enforcing unreasonably difficult restrictions. Or, when a speed limit is raised by five or ten miles per hour, studies show that people will still drive just slightly over it, pushing the boundary.

---

* Don't tell your teenager about the study conducted at UC Berkeley, which found that a teenager's brain is "not capable of the kind of reasoning that allows most grown-ups to make rational decisions." That's a pretty good excuse. "Sorry, Dad, I got a D because my brain chose a game of Halo over homework."

† For many marketers, the eighteen- to thirty-five-year-old male audience is an extremely important part of the mix. If you want to promote yourself to guys, strongly consider vice in your repertoire.

What lessons could we draw from DARE? When we sincerely intend to create constructive structure, could we be triggering negative behaviors instead?

How to Encourage Someone to *Want* to Break Your Rules

Let's play a game. Say we want to activate vice. How might we go about that? If you pull the heavyweight vice levers below, you could stand back and watch the backlash.

- First, enforce rigidly black-and-white behavioral codes. Speak in absolute terms such as "never," "always," and "no." Develop a strict, authoritative relationship, with punishment that seems unjustifiable. Exaggerate negative consequences. ("If you kiss a boy, you'll get pregnant.")
- Give a firm "no" without a reasonable reason why. For most people, being told that they can't do something is like a matador's red cape to a bull. Make people want to rebel, so they can prove their independence against you.
- Fail to establish trust. Present your lessons without any familiar context or figures.
- Finally, use the "unopened black box" method we saw at the beginning of this section: Trigger mystique by tempting someone, by giving them just a peek without any further explanation. Tell them what *not* to do, without telling them *why* they shouldn't do it.

How to Encourage Someone to Ignore Vice, and Follow *Your* Message

Now let's go in the opposite direction. How could you discourage vice, and encourage smarter choices? To overcome vice, adjust three other triggers: decrease mystique, and increase power and trust.

Start by decreasing the mystique trigger. Answer questions with open communication. Offer an honest appraisal of consequences. Don't allow secrets to build intrigue or confusion. The more transparent you are, the less mystique can lure someone away from your message.

Next, make your group feel more powerful, by giving them control of some aspect of their environment. Encourage mutual respect, rather than a master/servant dynamic.

Most important, invest a great deal of time and energy in the trust trigger, making your group feel they can rely upon you. The more people *trust* what they're being told, and the more they *trust* the person giving them this information, the more likely they are to follow it.

One last note. The father of analytical psychology, Carl Jung, wrote, "The word 'happiness' would lose its meaning if it were not balanced by sadness." Similarly, the word "virtue" would lose its meaning if not balanced by vice. Keep it all in perspective, balancing virtue and vice. Once you get extremist on either end, the pendulum goes a-swingin'.

In this chapter so far, we've delved into hard-core vices: smuggling, pornography, and illegal drug use, not to mention bad reality TV. These examples, while a pleasant way to pass the time, might not appeal to a happily middle-of-the-road perspective. What is vice's role in decision making for the more conservative among us?

Give a Wink

Each trigger changes behavior in a unique way. A message with lust draws people in, because they crave a sensory experience. A message with prestige elevates itself above the rest. A message with alarm prods people to act quickly. These have clear application for companies. How, and when, does vice apply?

Unconventional companies and "challenger brands" often benefit from stirring up new energy around a topic. Mid-sized, niche, or emerging brands lack certain advantages that the eight-hundred-pound gorilla enjoys. Their survival depends upon their ability to disrupt perceptions and force reevaluation. With smaller budgets, they often require free PR and buzz, which benefits from controversy.

Category leaders such as Fortune 100 corporations or incumbent politicians generally envision different fascination goals for themselves. These leaders tend to have long-standing relationships, with highly ingrained customer habits and decades-long messages, and want to maintain the status quo. They use vice less often, focusing instead on triggers that maintain established norms: prestige, power, or trust. However, ignoring vice isn't always the wisest choice.

Used wisely, vice can offer a fresh sense of unexpectedness to an otherwise straightforward message. This is true even for the biggest corporations, such as Wal-Mart and General Electric. Like the mystique trigger, vice piques our curiosity to know more. And like the alarm trigger, it surprises us with a potential change in direction, grabbing our instant attention.

How Could a More Traditional Brand Employ Vice?

Certain people and brands (Tabasco, Wonderbra, singer Lady GaGa) tempt consumers with a taste of forbidden fruit. But what about a more traditional brand message? How might you take a product that's a fungible commodity, is defined by utility, or is stuck in a parity category, and somehow make it fascinating?

- If you're a mattress company: What if you named your pillow-top mattress the "Sunday Morning Sleep-In"?
- If you're a credit card company: What if your rewards program had a "sin package" that only members over twenty-one could join? Instead of regular points, would you offer credits for online gambling?
- If you're an electronics company: What if your headphones included a secret "road to deafness" volume setting?
- If you're a car dealership: What if your car company invested in a private U.S. autobahn that let you drive as fast as you wanted after purchase?

Tweaking Expectations

To see how we might apply vice to your environment, start by tweaking established expectations. That's what Maya Lin did.

War memorials are *always* alabaster white. At least they were until 1982, when a young, unknown student named Maya Lin beat fourteen hundred others competing to design the Vietnam Veterans Memorial. Her black reflective granite wall created protests of outrage. Not only was the monument not white, it was also not a towering obelisk.

"The Wall" has become not only a powerful and beloved tribute, but profoundly connective, affecting its visitors through the interaction between their reflection in the black granite with the names of the fifty-eight thousand dead engraved into the stone. Lin won the design contest by creating a monument that not only commemorated, but broke with conventional norms in a category.

Allow Your Audience's Imagination to Do the Work for You

While a sliver of habanero chile pepper can pique interest, the intensity of a thick slice can turn off or repel. Rather than focusing solely on vice, use it as one ingredient in an overall strategy.

Subtlety works best. Over-explanation, justification, and backtracking all kill vice as surely as flipping on fluorescent lights in a candlelit restaurant and watching cockroaches scurry from view.

Combining Vice with Other Triggers

Two triggers, used together, can be stronger than either one alone. Just as sliced green apples complement a crisp sauvignon blanc, certain triggers perfectly pair together with vice. A few time-tested favorites:

Vice + Alarm

Box office sales prove the winning partnership of vice and alarm. Depravity, evil, and gore lure in crowds. While other Hollywood movie genres slip, the horror genre takes in hundreds of millions without traditional star vehicles. *Friday the 13th* has eleven movies in the franchise and a TV series. (If Jason isn't your thing, you can choose from six *Saw* films, five *Child's Play*, eight *Hellraiser*, and six *Texas Chainsaw Massacre* films.)

Vice + Power

When a mogul lights up a fat Cuban cigar in a nonsmoking restaurant, he seems to imply that for him, ordinary rules simply do not apply. Same for corporate con men at Enron, or recall Leona Helmsley's infamous "Only the little people pay taxes." With power, studies show, comes an entitlement to break the rules. If power makes people more likely to indulge in unre-strained behavior, it's certainly a highly compatible partner to vice, which tempts us to bend the rules.

Social psychologist Deborah Gruenfeld studies the effect that power has upon powerful people. A *Stanford Business* ar-ticle by Marguerite Rigoglioso shares her research. As people experience power, says Gruenfeld, they become *disinhibited*: less likely to control themselves and their behavior, less con-cerned with what others think of them, and more likely to flaunt cultural constraints and consequences. "When people experience power, they stop trying to control themselves; they forget that there are social consequences."

Vice + Lust

When vice meets lust, naughty things happen. Just ask Hugh Grant. As you might recall, Grant, the charming rogue movie star, was infamously interrupted in an oral dalliance with a Hollywood prostitute named Divine Brown. For many, this was especially perplexing in light of the fact that not only was Hugh Grant wealthy enough to rendezvous with someone who lived in the 310 area code, but at the time his long-time part-ner was über-supermodel Elizabeth Hurley. It's unclear why Grant was attracted to Ms. Brown,* but it's clear why he was attracted to the combination of vice + lust. Even if your audi-ence isn't *deviant*, you probably want them to *deviate*—from their current behavior, at least.

---

* For this disrupted paradise by the dashboard light, Ms. Brown (née Thompson) charged Hugh Grant only $60 cash. However, from the ensuing publicity sur-rounding the arrest, she reportedly earned $1.6 million. In a newspaper article titled "Hugh's Divine Intervention," Brown describes that her rendezvous with Grant bought her a four-bedroom home and private school education for her children. Not bad for a night's work.

. . . .

THE PURPOSE OF A message with vice isn't to lure your audience into sin, but rather to lure them away from their standard choices. A message with vice encourages people to change their patterns and try something different: a most useful tactic for anyone who wants to change ingrained beliefs or behavior.

If you're interested in building a long-term relationship, vice isn't your trigger. Trust is. After peeking at mystique, alerting to alarm, and flirting with vice, let's now find out how to build meaningful and authentic relationships over time.

Trust

Why We're Loyal to Reliable Options

Hum a few bars of "O Come All Ye Faithful," sip your eggnog, and gather round the fireplace to roast chestnuts, kids. It's time to tell the story of how the trust trigger brought us our traditional holiday classic *It's a Wonderful Life*.

Upon its release in 1946, *It's a Wonderful Life* wasn't quite the success it is today. Actually, it flopped. Soundly. Earnings didn't come close to the cost of production, the studio was disappointed, and the director, Frank Capra, was criticized and humiliated. The holiday movie seemed destined to fade into obscurity. But then, serendipitously, trust came into play.

In 1974, the film's copyright protection slipped. It became public domain. Now, television stations could air *It's a Wonderful Life* for free. And air it they did. Every year, the movie played throughout the Christmas season. Families gathered to watch. Children grew up with Jimmy Stewart and the angels. Americans saw the same images year after year. Jimmy Stewart and the angels became emblazoned on our collective concept of holidays, hope, and American optimism. From a marketing perspective, the movie has become an ingrained part of the Christmas "brand architecture" along with gift-wrapped toys, caroling, and the colors red and green. It's a tradition.

Yet like many traditions, one might argue, this one succeeds not because it's the *highest-quality* option, but because it's the most *familiar*. Familiarity and repetition have turned the movie into a fascinating holiday message. We love *It's a Wonderful Life* because, unlike the audiences in 1946, we know it.

What Is Trust?

The other six triggers can fascinate us in a short time frame. The sound of an ambulance siren instantly triggers alarm. A magazine article's provocative title sucks us in with mystique. One glance at the latest iPhone summons lust. Trust, however, is fascination of a different sort. This trigger is more complex than the other six. It's more nuanced, more fragile, harder to earn, and much easier to lose. You can dabble in prestige, or experiment with power, but you can't dip in and out of trust. It must be established consistently.

Other triggers often guide our decision making by provoking us in some way. Alarm thrills us with immediacy or change. Mystique stimulates us with curiosity. Trust, however, guides everyday decision making in a different way: familiarity and comfort. For example, we choose to put on our favorite old college sweatshirt because we trust it to feel exactly the same as it has felt for years. We trust the opinions of our friends or acquaintances over that of a random stranger. We repeat family traditions, like watching *It's a Wonderful Life*, because they provide reassuring shared continuity for the group.

As we've seen, we're living in an ADD world. Even if we ourselves don't have ADD, we have to deal with fragmented schedules, competing demands, and priorities pulling our attention in different directions. Even our relationships change more frequently, making everyday life feel more scattered. In the face of overwhelming stimuli, the most trusted options relax and reassure us. Continuity makes us feel safe.

How to establish and enhance trust? Five pillars for trust: Become familiar. Repeat and retell. Be authentic. Accelerate trust in a shorter time frame. And "un-fascinate" an unhealthy message. Messages will use different pillars depending upon their stage and purpose, but as our strongest pillar in relationships, drawing upon one or more of these pillars can win the battle for attention.

Become Familiar

The word "familiar" comes from *familia*, meaning family. Family is more than just an emotional bond, and so is familiarity. Neurochemically, there's a lot going on with familiarity. Our minds look for patterns. When we recognize them, we not only rely on them, but also develop preferences based on pattern repetition. Our brains use these patterns to map everything we see, hear, and experience in order to establish an expectation for the future.

The Exposure Effect

In 1876, Gustav Fechner described this phenomenon, calling it the "exposure effect." The more we're exposed to something or someone, the more we trust it. And the more we *like* it. Scientists have since used the exposure effect to describe why we might like a song more after hearing it a few times, why we feel more comfortable around friends than strangers, and why we're inclined to feel as though we personally know celebrities we see frequently. Consistent and repeated exposure to a celebrity such as Will Smith or Oprah Winfrey makes us more likely to trust them, and *like* them, because their images have created a neurochemical pattern on our brains.

These patterns can slowly accumulate over the course of years, as with *It's a Wonderful Life*. But does that mean only adults experience trust? Do we experience the exposure effect early in life?

McNuggets, Milk, and the Golden Arches

McDonald's earns fascination through many triggers. The sight, smell, and taste of a Big Mac build lust. Their fries rouse vice with sodium-laden goodness. And through repetition of messaging and consistency of experience, they earn trust.

It doesn't take long for McDonald's to build trust in young diners. In a study designed to show the effects of marketing on young children, researchers at the Stanford University School of Medicine and Lucile Packard Children's Hospital presented children ages three to five with two different sets of chicken nuggets. They wrapped one set of nuggets in McDonald's packaging, and the other in plain, unmarked packaging. Which group of nuggets tasted better? they asked. The twist: The packaging was different, but the nuggets themselves were exactly the same.

Overwhelmingly, the young patrons rated the McDonald's branded food as tasting better than the unbranded food—even though the food was *exactly* the same. Thomas Robinson, director of the Center for Healthy Weight at Packard Children's Hospital, reports, "Kids don't just ask for food from McDonald's, they actually believe that the chicken nugget they think is from McDonald's tastes better than an identical, unbranded nugget." Not only did kids prefer the flavor of branded nuggets, but also the taste of menu items not normally associated with McDonald's: carrots, milk, and apple juice when these foods were presented in McDonald's-branded packaging. By age three, their taste buds were already "tricked" into imagining superior taste.

To fascinate diners with trust, Mickey D's doesn't just invest in becoming the most familiar option. It also allows people to know what to expect from each encounter by maintaining predictability.

Maintaining Predictability

Earning trust demands an investment of time and effort, because predictability requires a guaranteed certainty. Trusted brands carefully pay attention to detail, reinforcing consistency between expectations they set and results they deliver. In return, the reward for earning trust is a big one: loyalty.

Loyalty acts as a rudder of decision making, because in certain circumstances, we want to know *exactly* what to expect. Surprises aren't fun when it comes to an auto manufacturer's warranty, auto-deposit of a paycheck, or the skill of our cardiac surgeon. In these types of relationships, we seek reliable options. Safety is paramount and excitement is bad, so we're drawn to stability. Year after year, we might return to the same accountant not for her keen fashion sense or witty banter, but because we don't have to worry if our 1040 form will pass muster.

"I'll Have the Usual"

We order the same dish in a restaurant over and over not because it's surprising, but the opposite: We know and love it.

Once we know what to expect from a brand, they've already done much of the decision-making heavy lifting for us. McDonald's applies this premise to its message, as do many of the most established companies.

Trusted brands reliably deliver specific qualities: In the morning, we can wake up and put on a navy blue Brooks Brothers jacket knowing it won't look passé, get into our assuredly safe Volvo, and drive to any Starbucks in the country to enjoy the same cup of coffee. At work we can sit at an ergonomic Aeron chair and stylish Herman Miller desk, writing with the Sharpie pen that won't wash off. On the way home from work, while listening to a Miles Davis song that we know will be cool, we can pick up a dinner we know will be healthy at Whole Foods. After work, we can see a Francis Ford Coppola movie that we know will be epic, and perhaps crack open an Anheuser-Busch beer, which, we're about to find out, has been approved by a panel of predictability experts.

Anheuser-Busch takes predictability seriously. This company's quality control might be renamed "predictability control." Members of an elite panel ensure the consistency of the beer's flavor from brewery to brewery, day to day. To guarantee uniformity, samples from each of the fifteen breweries are flown into the St. Louis headquarters, served to the tasters in identically selected glasses that have been cleaned precisely with filtered water. The panel samples every ingredient, including air, which they bubble through water and sip. Because of this, consumers can trust that every beer, from every brewery, tastes the same.

Over the years, traditional marketing has built these companies into familiar friends. Even if we've never driven a Volvo or worn a Brooks Brothers, we develop expectations based on their reputations.

The more predictable a message, the more we rely on it. These brands demand very little learning curve, reassuring us by recognizing our expectations, and reliably satisfying them. Trusted messages are also consistent, with very little conflicting input, because inconsistency breaks trust. To build consistency, repeat your message, and retell your story.

Repeat and Retell

Many organizations use consistency to influence behavior, but one did so with devastating effectiveness. Instead of selling a product, this organization sold an ideology. Instead of ingraining beliefs about a store, it ingrained beliefs about life and death. And millions of people followed the message, as horrible as the message was. How did this organization use trust?

How Did the Nazis Instill Their Message?[*]

As we saw earlier, if an organization wants to persuade followers through trust, it must deliver a very consistent, reliable message. If people hear that message repeatedly and consistently, and if that message has few deviations and little conflicting information around it, they "trust" it. In the absence of conflicting input, even a false message will be trusted.

If there are *opposing* viewpoints, however—if an audience hears a *variety* of messages—then as a whole, they're more likely to start asking questions. They form opinions and make their own decisions, becoming less likely to blindly trust any one specific message. The audience fragments, trusting different messages.

---

[*] A difficult question. But to quote George Santayana's words that are inscribed on the walls of the Auschwitz concentration camp, "The one who does not remember history is bound to live through it again."

If you're a propagandist, this presents a real problem. Propagandists don't want opposing viewpoints. That is especially true of a propagandist whose message violates his audience's deeper beliefs. For these communicators, it is not enough to merely repeat the message—dissenters must also be squelched.

Propagandists use information control to enforce exact consistency. They monitor every possible piece of information their audience might absorb, rigorously reinforcing their agendas while going to great lengths to prevent outside contradicting influences. No matter how illogical or heinous their argument may be, followers are almost forced to trust it. It's all they know.

Nazi propaganda chief Joseph Goebbels was a master of manipulating trust through consistent repetition. He wrote, "If you tell a lie big enough and keep repeating it, people will eventually come to believe it. . . . It thus becomes vitally important for the State to use all of its powers to repress dissent." Adolf Hitler, in his autobiography *Mein Kampf* ("My Struggle"), instructs that the purpose of propaganda is to attract the attention of the crowd, "so skillfully that everyone will be convinced that the fact is real," by not overestimating the intelligence of the masses. He summarizes, "The greater the lie, the greater the chance that it will be believed." Make the lie big, make it simple, keep saying it, and eventually they will believe it.

All Propaganda Is Marketing

Hitler even applied this to marketing, reinforcing a need for absolute declaration: "What, for example, would we say about a poster that was supposed to advertise a new soap and that described other soaps as 'good'? We would only shake our heads. Exactly the same applies to political advertising."

In a quote that could just as easily come from a Marketing 101 class, Hitler teaches, "The art of propaganda lies in understanding the emotional ideas of the great masses and finding, through a psychologically correct form, the way to the attention and thence to the heart of the broad masses." Marketing isn't necessarily propaganda. All propaganda, however, is marketing.

Trust doesn't demand a moral absolute—only absolute consistency. Repeating a message and retelling a story will drill in blind trust. However, to build a genuine relationship with an audience, a message must reflect sincerity and authenticity.

Be Authentic

From Gymborees to mothers' teas, parents gush about Baby Einstein videos. And what's not to like? Plop your child (whether infant, toddler, or kindergartener) in front of the TV while you step away to do dishes or (gasp!) enjoy some free time. In your absence, your little darling only grows smarter and more verbally proficient. What a guilt-free parenting indulgence! Even President Bush praised the company. But . . . oh, wait, what's this? A study published in the *Journal of Pediatrics* reveals, "For every hour per day spent watching Baby Einstein DVDs and videos, infants age eight to 16 months understood an average of six to eight fewer words than those who did not watch them."*

Villains, Heroes, and Other Personal Brands

We measure how much we "trust" something by comparing our expectations against deviations. The more similar

---

* My own kids are doomed.

something is to our expectations, the more we count on it. Reputations confirm this.

We trust good guys to be good. (Notice how few fairy tales illustrate Prince Charming embezzling from the royal coffers.) We also "trust" Darth Vader, Cruella de Vil, and Caligula to be bad. We revel in the evil of Heath Ledger's Joker, and the innocence of Forrest Gump. If an established character deviates sharply from his persona, we're confused, even disappointed.

In the case of superagent Ari Gold on HBO's *Entourage*, unpredictability might make for interesting TV. But in the workplace, consistency is the cornerstone of a reputation built around trust. In the office, just as in the movies, predictable behavior builds a reputation, but erratic action unravels the pattern.* Reputations influence decision making. People make trust judgments based on comparisons to past experiences. If your success relies on instant gratification or surprise, then use trust at your leisure. However, if your success relies on trust, then you must, without question, deliver what people expect. The more specific your promise, the more urgent the need to deliver. We're indignant if a FedEx shows up late (when it absolutely, positively needed to be there overnight), or if a Timex watch takes a licking but doesn't keep ticking. Brands that fail to live up to their raison d'être earn negative fascination: bad word of mouth. The brands that we consistently trust are those that fulfill expectations.

---

* Note: "Consistent" doesn't necessarily mean "good." Trust builds a strong expectation of *future* behavior based on *past* behavior. Now, that behavior could be bad. That college buddy who always runs half an hour late, but you still meet him out for drinks anyway? You've figured out his patterns, and can accurately judge his behavior. His tardiness might annoy you, but won't surprise you.

Flavor of the Month

Tempestuous by nature, fads can feel sexy and exciting. They whip up exaggerated, even zealous fascination. Some triggers can benefit from fads, especially lust, prestige, or alarm. However, trends are a fickle mistress. They're difficult to maneuver or maintain.

For iconic people and companies, fads can erode credibility. Or worse, damage trust. Trusted messages are not mercurial. Neon-yellow leggings or a slick fauxhawk might do many things, but earning trust likely isn't among them. For a retailer, sustaining the same message might sound easy enough, but the reality is that tastes change, economies change, and companies change. Sometimes, it's easy to give in to the temptation of cashing in on a fad.

Fashion Victim or Fashion Victor?

A quintessential classic, the Tiffany & Co. logo is engraved into 170 years of exclusivity. Yet in the late 1990s, Tiffany's lower-priced line of silver jewelry took off as a must-have sensation among teenage girls. In particular, one $110 charm bracelet became a must-have fashion item. Other brands would rejoice in the brisk sales, yet Tiffany executives knew these trinkets could make the brand too accessible for older, wealthier patrons. As the company's stock prices rose, so did the concerns.

In a controversial move, Tiffany raised prices on the silver pieces to put the brakes on this trend. This decision probably lost short-term profits from shoppers wanting an affordable look, but preserved prestige from the company's long-term wealthy base.

It's a risk to remain unchanged. Ruts are sticky. But for

companies that rely on long-standing trust as a primary trigger, every message must communicate stability.*

Contradictory Input Kills Trust

We're wired to attach our own security and safety to the idea of trust, so when those bonds are broken, we feel threatened. Broken trust can have disastrous effects, requiring serious effort, time, and a savvy plan to rebuild.

A situation that no homeowner has ever, ever faced:† a contractor who finishes a remodeling job later than expected. If a contractor promises to have a remodel finished in one month, but you're living in your bedroom for three months, they've created a contradiction between their message (completion promised in a month) and their results (completion in three months), thereby introducing a dissonance between what they *say* and *do*. Instead of trust, the contractor is more likely triggering alarm around deadlines. In the workplace, loss of fascination can translate to loss of a job, especially when deadlines and budgets are tight.

Breaking and Rebuilding Trust

Everyone makes mistakes. Even with the best intentions, messages can turn out differently than planned, especially after making a mistake. They point out the break in expectations, in order to rebuild patterns of trust.

For Odwalla, the natural juice company, trust is a main trigger of the brand. Along with lust (for their juicy flavors), the

---

* In twenty years, when those teenage girls acquire the spending power for lavish gold and diamonds, they won't associate the Tiffany & Co. logo with the one attached to that cute little sterling silver trinket they wore back in high school.

† Dripping sarcasm.

company built itself on absolute freshness, without pasteurization. But since there was no pasteurization to kill bacteria on the apples, the apples needed to be picked only directly from the trees. A worker in the grove apparently took a fruit from the ground, and the resulting E. coli outbreak killed a little girl named Anna. Rather than explaining or hiding, Odwalla worked directly with everyone in the supply chain. They removed all fruit juices from the shelves, and within just five weeks of the recall, developed a "flash pasteurization" method of preserving fresh flavor, for both quality and consumer safety.

Odwalla broke trust, then repaired it. And they did so on an accelerated time frame. If you don't have years to build trust, it is possible to speed the process by weaving existing associations in with your message. Even without a 170-year-old reputation on your side, like Tiffany & Co.

Accelerate Trust

A message can become established fairly quickly, as Hitler's did, through repetition without contradictory input. In most cases, however, an enduringly trusted message takes time to build. The message doesn't need to be biggest, or best, or first of its kind: The eventual success of *It's a Wonderful Life* showed how retelling a story makes it more trusted over time.

Repetition alone is rarely enough to make a message fascinating. To earn trust, ideally the message itself will extend over time. To accelerate trust, however, a message can tap into *values* that extend over time.*

---

* Consider your own family's traditions: They usually are not focused on the "best" foods or the "biggest" gestures, but rather on a sense of continuity that draws upon your home, your shared history, your favorite activities, and time spent around your kitchen table.

Reinventing Cues from the Past

Yesterday's tired facts can be reinvented anew. And just about anything from your past is fair game. Colt 45, the malt liquor favored by the urban poor, turned a flinch-worthy truth into a street-smart marketing tool. Instead of hiding from the fact that the oversized bottles are usually carried in small brown paper bags, they created cool hand-drawn ads printed directly on small brown paper bags. The campaign used its heritage to do the seemingly impossible: reposition Colt 45 to hipster drinkers.

Companies occasionally rebuild trust by going back into their own history and bringing back old marketing devices. Maxwell House returned to "Good to the last drop," Star-Kist tuna reintroduced Charlie the Tuna, and Burger King invited us to once again have it our way.

Companies lacking in perennial trust cues often simply borrow someone else's. Senekot laxatives borrowed James Brown's "I Feel Good," and Viagra regaled us with "Viva Viagra." Sea-Bond Denture Adhesive brought back "Bye Bye Love." If a song isn't quite exactly right off-the-rack, many TV commercials take poetic license (as long as they pay to license the song): Luvs diapers paraphrases the Beatles' "All You Need Is Luvs." And Kraft Cheese Crumbles brought us their version of "Unbelievable," the hum-worthy "Crumbelievable."*Are dead celebrities off-limits for conjuring trust cues? Hmm. Maybe not always the best idea. Using old footage, amid a 1997 outcry, a Dirt Devil commercial featured Fred Astaire dancing with a vacuum cleaner. Orville Redenbacher died in

---

* Reportedly, a hemorrhoid cream was about to use Johnny Cash's "Ring of Fire" for a TV commercial, until Cash's family exerted their good taste.

1995, but through the wonders of computer graphics, a 2007 commercial featured him holding an iPod while touting his microwave popcorn.

Using Familiar Cues for Introductions

Remember the "exposure effect"? We're drawn to people and situations that feel familiar. They fit a pattern we already know. This logic explains why "Crumbelievable" probably tested so well in focus groups. And it explains why we're more likely to extend trust to something that's similar to what we know.

By linking a new message to one that's already firmly trusted, we can shorten the time frame needed to develop trust. Real estate professionals often use the scent of baking bread or cookies when showing a home to buyers, because these nostalgic scents cue unconscious memories for many buyers. The scents bring familiar cues to an unfamiliar environment, making it seem more immediately homelike.

"Unfascinate" an Unhealthy Message

Can a message become *too* fascinating—so fascinating that for a certain group of people, it's no longer possible to logically evaluate it? Cults are too fascinating, and so are ultra-extremist political groups. They influence to the point of brainwashing, with messages that can overwhelm all other choices. Embedded with trust, these messages can be extremely difficult to neutralize.

The Darker Side of Trust

It is possible to break an unhealthy decision-making cycle by replacing one message with another. The unhealthy message must first become "unfastened," and replaced by a new, healthier message.

In the section on vice, we saw how the DARE anti-drug program has the unexpected result of increasing the likelihood of drug use among teens. And we learned that trust overcomes vice: When trusted peers, rather than strangers, teach prevention, the anti-drug message becomes far more effective. Trust can deter, or even reverse, negative behavior caused by other triggers.

Unhealthy Trust

Just as trust encourages us to gravitate to a familiar image rather than an unfamiliar one, so do we gravitate to familiar messages. And we gravitate to familiar messages whether they're healthy or not. Fast food is an ingrained message, and as a consequence, obesity is a negative consequence of trust. For those who've grown up with fast food as a regular, established part of their dining repertoire, fast food is a comfortable, reliable staple.

A few pages ago, we looked at young kids' learned preference for McDonald's branded chicken nuggets. As the trust attachment to fast food grows, so do the health risks. We've all seen the news reports and articles on childhood obesity. The numbers keep getting worse: According to the Centers for Disease Control and Prevention, the number of overweight or obese children ages two to nineteen years old has tripled since 1980.

But let's be fair. Assuming we could hide McDonald's signs from our children, and never allow them to watch TV commercials or play with the Happy Meal toys, would they choose rhubarb over a candy bar? Taking it a step further, assuming both unhealthy and healthy options were equally available, would kids pick kale over fries? Can healthy food ever hope to compete with fast-food culture? Is it possible for our society to win the battle against childhood obesity—a battle against billion-dollar marketing budgets, against the body's natural appetite for salt and fat and sugar, and against even the force of a deeply ingrained trigger of trust?

In one little schoolyard parking lot, fast food is starting to lose the battle.

The Edible Schoolyard

When it comes to food shopping and consumption, there's been a fundamental shift in the United States since World War II. Instead of purchasing food directly from farmers, we've shifted to a processed model, purchasing food from manufacturers such as fast-food restaurants. As a result, most children have very little experience with food in its original, unprocessed state.

One school is changing the rules, giving kids a "happy meal" of a different sort. This lunch doesn't come in a box printed with puzzles, but rather from a garden planted by the kids themselves. Alice Waters, a major proponent of the organic food movement who is credited with developing California Cuisine, piloted the Edible Schoolyard. Waters started the program in 1994 in Berkeley, an outgrowth of the Chez Panisse Foundation, at the Martin Luther King Jr. Middle School.*
Students turned the school's parking lot into a garden, or an

---

* The Edible Schoolyard is, ironically, just thirty-eight miles north of the location of the McNuggets study at Lucile Packard Children's Hospital. On the drive from the children's hospital to the Edible Schoolyard, there are three McDonald's drive-throughs, in case you get hungry.

"edible schoolyard." Teachers and students cleared the land and developed a garden to teach kids about the entire process of how food comes from the earth to their plates. Kids don't just *eat* the food; they *experience* it. And they start to choose it over unhealthy food.

In a phone interview, Carolyn Federman, director of development at the Chez Panisse Foundation, described how the program "has shown that if you offer children a new dish, there's no better than a fifty-fifty chance they will choose it. But if they've been introduced to the dish ahead of time, and if they have helped prepare it, they will all want to try it." The kids say, for example, "I've learned that vegetables are better than I thought."

Banning unhealthy practices, or rejecting negative beliefs, will only spark vice, creating "forbidden fruit." But applying principles from the Edible Schoolyard, we might turn around negative habits or beliefs by replacing those beliefs with a new set of trusted experiences.

Lessons to Learn and Apply from the Edible Schoolyard

At some point, many of us face the difficult task of reversing a deeply ingrained opinion or belief. By identifying a new positive message, and introducing a variety of new ways to *experience* that message, we can start to loosen the grip of the old one. People learn by doing, because it ingrains new trust beliefs and habits in a variety of ways.

For the Edible Schoolyard program, for instance, food is an academic subject. Kids translate vegetable names from one language to another in Spanish class; in math class they convert grams to ounces; and in history class they learn about indigenous cultures and the origins of recipes. Go beyond rational data, and instead provoke creativity and emotion around your intended message. Cumulatively, these experiences fascinate by building a new trust.

Trust for Beginners

This most valuable of all triggers rarely comes quickly or easily. Tiffany demonstrated how difficult it is to maintain authenticity over time, requiring great effort and expense. If you're new to the trust trigger, and believe it's worth the investment, take a lesson from trusted people and companies.

When introducing yourself, find ways that your message can feel instantly familiar. Pinpoint shared values with your audience, since people bond more quickly with others who have similar values and traits to their own.

Identify the patterns you want to fascinate others with. If you build upon them and stick to them, trust will build gradually and naturally over time. In the meantime, while trust builds, activate another trigger to generate fascination: prestige and power are trust's closest substitutes.

Until this point, we've been playing with triggers in abstract theory. Time to talk more tangibly about your own message, as it lives in the real world, with Part III, "The Fascination Plan of Attack." We'll poke and prod at your brand to find hidden gems and potential challenges. Applying the grand total of everything we've learned up to this point, we'll create your "badges" and "bell curves" in a creative process, and we'll apply the Gold Hallmarks to your own message.

Along the way, we'll pause to consider an $8,200 cocktail, a postmortem tattoo, and, oh, those delightfully bright orange polyester Hooters shorts.

Ready? Let's get fascinating.

PART III

The Fascination
Plan of Attack

*How to Make Your Own Messages
More Fascinating*

In Part I, we saw *why* people become fascinated. In Part II, we learned *which* triggers fascinate. Now, we'll start to develop your plan to make your own message more fascinating.

Ideas Kept under Lock and Key

Fascinating ideas are precious. They can change the course of a company's revenue, or change the course of history. We sometimes treat ideas indelicately, as through they're worth little more than the paper upon which they're written. Early in my career, one experience taught the value of fascinating ideas.

In 1991, the world headquarters of TBWA Advertising was located at 292 Madison Avenue. This was back when a Madison Avenue address was still considered de rigueur for an agency's letterhead. TBWA exuded the untouchable cool of an international catwalk model: aloof, poreless, slightly bored, altogether intimidating. It was the summer of 1991, when the agency had recently debuted the iconic Absolut Vodka campaign and was now polishing its fame to blinding perfection. Entering the all-white lobby made one feel suddenly self-conscious, acutely aware of some otherwise irrelevant detail, such as the fact that the dry cleaner's seamstress had recently resewn a button in a slightly off-color thread.

Yet on the first day of my unpaid summer internship, walking into that lobby, I felt no intimidation whatsoever. Not because I possessed that same unattainable cool, but quite the opposite. I was too clueless even to have a clue of how clueless I was. Just two weeks earlier I'd graduated from college wearing my new $29.95 Thom McAn white pumps, my unruly hair gelled back into a Laura Ashley bow, and that internship was mine, all mine.

My first week, I heard a rumor that the creative department staff locked their file drawers at night. Why? So no one could steal their ideas. I was naïve, but not blind, and this intrigued me greatly. What kind of intellectual bullion could possibly fill those files? These same employees casually left personal valuables such as watches and cameras on their desks at night, yet neurotically locked their file drawers? Whatever lay inside those OfficeMax treasure chests, I wanted some of it.

Over the course of the summer, I learned (while fetching coffee) why writers and art directors kept their ideas under lock and key. Those scribbles and words, when applied against a client's specific marketing challenges, could seed an entire brand campaign. If the campaign launched, in addition to skyrocketing the careers of those behind it, it could generate hundreds of millions of dollars for the client, realign entire product categories, and become a pop culture hero. TBWA had recently done just this: their global Absolut phenomenon all began with one single, hand-drawn piece of paper.

Today, if you and I somehow discovered one of those locked

filing chests and jimmied it open to sell at the neighborhood pawnshop, we'd be mightily disappointed. The ideas would probably be worthless. An idea is only as valuable as its ability to solve a problem.* Those TBWA ideas, while priceless in 1991, are meaningless outside the context for which they were created. Alas, there is no underground black market for storyboards and media plans.

Ideas are precious, yes—but not in and of themselves. They don't live in a vacuum. They become precious only once they successfully answer a specific need; otherwise they're just scribbles.

Just as you can't solve your own problems with TBWA's ideas, the ideas in this book won't become truly valuable until you apply them to your own context, obstacles, and goals. There is no one-size-fits-all fascination plan. However, through applying best-in-class principles used by the most influential brands, a framework emerges: the Fascination Plan of Attack.

Three Stages for Your Plan of Attack
Accelerated Lessons and Exercises for You and Your Team
Stage 1: Evaluation
Stage 2: Development
Stage 3: Execution

In my consulting and workshops, I chart an immersive Plan of Attack with clients. However, today, since I'm *here* and you're *there*, and we're not in the same room together, this book will

---

* Many ad agencies have created cultural alchemy with a single precious idea. Imagine a cocktail napkin scribbled with "Just Do It," or the back of a sales receipt with the handwritten words, "Got Milk?" Ideas can begin anywhere, including the whiteboard in your conference room this afternoon.

give you the tools you need to begin. What follows is your fascination crash course, condensed into a manageable DIY process for you and your team. I recommend completing Stage 1, Evaluation, over the course of a full day, so that you can collect a snapshot without diving so deep that you lose perspective. Stage 2, Development, can take hours or years, depending on your needs. Again, I suggest a full day minimum on a specific message. Stage 3, Execution, is an ongoing process. It's worth spending a day discussing the opportunities and obstacles laid out here, but this should become a continual part of integrating fascination into your team's thinking.

Before you start getting ready to cram your own filing cabinets full of precious ideas, here are a few quick housekeeping items. First, it's unrealistic to think you'll motor through this whole curriculum at once, so consider doing this program as an intensive meeting over the course of two or three days. Next, document everything you generate, because ideas that seem unrealistic at first can be viable later. Finally, there must be snacks involved. (Go easy on the Red Bull, though.) All right then, let's begin.

The discussion, exercises, and questions that follow will help your team embark on three critical steps for innovation: Assess your current levels of fascination, create new forms of fascination, and then successfully apply potential ideas. First, we'll evaluate how effectively you're fascinating your audience.

Stage 1: Evaluation

How Fascinating Are Your Company and Message?

We've seen how fascination persuades people to do things they don't understand (cheating on diets or spouses), believe messages that don't make sense (chicken nuggets taste better if wrapped in McDonald's packaging), and buy things they don't even enjoy (Jägermeister, baby!). Unsurprisingly, then, this evaluation process might feel unfamiliar at first.

Here's the first difference between a traditional evaluation and our Plan of Attack: We won't be evaluating your own messages. As tempting as it might be to spend time examining what you do and say, that's fairly irrelevant here. Fascination lives not in your own communication to the world, but rather in how the world communicates *about you*. Sure, marketers used to control the message, but today, the market controls the message.

Messages take off and become fascinating through the six Gold Hallmarks introduced in Part I. By tweaking the Hallmarks, we can more easily use them to evaluate your own company and message. Take a deep breath, and a good, hard look. How is your company performing against these criteria?

Gold Hallmarks of a Fascinating Message

- Do we provoke strong and immediate emotional reactions?
- Do we create advocates?
- Are we "cultural shorthand" for a specific set of actions or values?
- Do we incite conversation?
- Do we force competitors to realign around us?
- Do we trigger social revolutions?

Let's take a moment to apply each.

Exercise: Evaluate Whether You're Provoking Strong and Immediate Emotional Reactions

The unfortunate reality is that most marketers set out to create messages that offend the fewest people. They're playing *not* to lose. Yet as we saw with world championship poker, Landmark Education, and Jay Gnospelius, strong and immediate reactions are a key characteristic of fascinating brands. Some reactions are positive, some not, but they do fascinate.

If you're not generating a negative reaction from *someone*, you're probably not fascinating *anyone*. List the reactions, both positive and negative, that you provoke.

Exercise: Evaluate Whether You're Creating Advocates

Your fans may be a small slice of your overall base, but they're the most passionate and vocal, and they'll participate in your marketing work. Fiskars (yes, that old scissors company) created a "crafting ambassadors" program called "Fisk-A-Teers." These scrapbooking aficionados and craft connoisseurs get to learn from one another, and the company gets an ongoing focus group of free research on potential new products, lifestyle insight, and new product ideas. Fiskars doesn't talk *to* its audience; instead, it gives the audience ways to connect through the brand.

Maker's Mark Bourbon Whisky harnesses the power of its greatest fans, allowing them to play an integral role in the growth of the brand. Each "ambassador" gets his own Maker's Mark barrel of whisky, marked with his name; the company sends regular updates about this personal barrel, with the opportunity to taste and purchase from this batch. Maker's Mark even provides ambassadors with business cards! These consumers aren't just consumers, they're activists. Can you create ambassadors? How would you reward them, inspire them, and support their communication with you, and with one another?

If you don't currently have a fan base for your message, challenge yourself with the following questions: What would it take to compel someone to pay for a T-shirt bearing your logo? What would it take to make people stand in line for hours to purchase your product? What would it take for people to pay double to obtain your product—even if the utility of the product didn't change? What would it take for your product to become so beloved that it never, ever went on sale?

Exercise: Evaluate Whether You're Embodying Specific Core Values

In an attempt to be all things to all people, most brands end up saying nothing to anyone. Fascinating companies earn attention by focusing on a specific message: Home Depot (do-it-yourself), Patagonia (sustainability), Target (accessible style), Nordstrom (overachieving service), or De Beers (romantic expression). Tiffany & Co. made a tough decision to reduce their line of trendy silver pieces, but in doing so, preserved trust and prestige.

Even tiny details represent bigger core values. Pret A Manger, a gourmet take-out chain, stirs its granola by hand with a four-foot-long wooden oar. Sure, they could far more easily stir it with a mechanical mixer, but according to Pret's "slow food" beliefs, this would damage their oatmeal's flavor and texture. That wooden oar stirs not only the oatmeal, but also our imagination. That oar tidbit, while not advertised or promoted anywhere, tells us that all of Pret's food will be as homemade as a New York deli's can be.

Ask Yourself:

- Do you represent such a distinct point of view that you can stand as a symbol for certain values?
- What's the one essential quality without which your brand would not survive?
- A more challenging question: What core values is your brand so committed to that it would be willing to go out of business before sacrificing them? (If you have trouble with this question, the alarm trigger should be activating right about now.)

Exercise: Evaluate Whether You're "Cultural Shorthand" for a Set of Actions or Values

Early Volkswagen Bug and Porsche owners would wave to one another, bonding over their shared choice in cars. Airstream motor homes have ID numbers, so Airstream owners can tell who just passed them. People identify with fascinating brands: They identify themselves, their opinions, and their community. (As the commercial says, "Are you a Mac, or PC?")

Ask Yourself:

- How do customers use your product or message to tell the world about themselves and their point of view?

Exercise: Evaluate Whether You're Inciting Conversations

People don't want to connect with *brands*. They want to connect with *one another*. The U.S. military created a way for members of its target audience to connect with one another over a product. When the number of military recruits dropped, the military started conversations among potential recruits by creating a video game. Future Force Company Commander, or F2C2, portrays the nation's futuristic military as an invulnerable high-tech organization, giving its consumers (teenage boys) a carefully controlled glimpse of battle. It doesn't matter if you agree with the game, you can't ignore why it got so many potential recruits talking, and connecting.

The more people become fascinated by you and your message, the more they want to interact with you: playing with you, talking about you, learning from you, and above all, connecting with you and then with one another.

Ask Yourself:

- What opportunities do you create for people to connect with one another?

Exercise: Evaluate Whether You're Forcing Competitors to Realign

Zappos.com forced its competitors, and its category, to realign. For many consumers, shopping online had two big barriers: the potential inconvenience of returns, and potential shipping costs. To lower the alarm trigger, Zappos offers free shipping both ways, thereby killing two risks with one stone. Zappos.com also triggers power (by giving consumers more control), with a highly visual site and multiple product shots (for the gratification of lust). Prestige enters the mix with "Zappos Couture," featuring Vivienne Westwood, Moschino, and other decidedly un-Zappos-like designers. And since we're talking about women and shoes, it's also a vice combination! This online model, while deceptively simple, defines its category through innovation with multiple triggers. In 2009, Amazon bought the company for $928 million, leaving many competitors flat-footed.

Ask Yourself:

- How could you communicate so distinctively that your innovations turn into your consumers' expectations? How can you set your competitors on the defensive?

Exercise: Evaluate Whether You're Tapping Into, or Triggering, Social Revolutions

When people become fascinated, they merge with larger groups of people fascinated by the same message. These groups can do much of your work for you, inciting others to join a bigger cultural movement. Harley-Davidson revolutionized a category, and sparked a revolution. Jim Nelson, executive creative director at ad agency Carmichael Lynch, explains that in the sixties, the public had an extremely negative opinion of motorcycle riding. To refute this, *Cycle World* magazine published an article claiming that 99 percent of bikers were law-abiding, responsible citizens—the other 1 percent of outlaw bikers were giving the rest a bad name. Harley riders took that 1 percent as a badge of honor, calling themselves the "One Percenters." In response, Honda came out with a campaign that said, "You meet the nicest people on a Honda." Harley didn't back down on its message. These riders didn't want to be nice, they wanted to ride.*

Social revolutions aren't once-in-a-decade events. They're happening constantly, every single day: from political beliefs, use

---

* A man owned both a bar and a Harley. During his life, he collected several large Harley tattoos on his back and shoulders. When he died, his son had the tattoos removed, tanned, and framed in the bar. I'm uncertain if this is a positive for patrons at the bar; however, it is good proof that Harley fascinates.

of technology, fashion, and consumption of media, to local communities and family structure. Even if you don't trigger a social revolution, as Harley did, you can certain tap into cultural changes.

Ask Yourself:

- How can your message capitalize on emerging changes? For instance, could your advertising pinpoint a new trend, and use it to your advantage?
- Could you tie your message into what people are already doing and saying around a specific cause?
- What groups, communities, and tribes could your message excite and activate, so that they champion your message as part of their own?

Identifying Your Primary Trigger

You're already using triggers (whether you intend to or not, and whether you want to or not). By now you probably have an idea of your primary fascination trigger—the one that most closely embodies the way in which you fascinate others. You might also have an idea of your secondary triggers. While clarifying your triggers, and the ways in which you use them, it helps to print out a list of the seven triggers to have in front of you:

LUST is the desire or craving for sensory gratification.
MYSTIQUE lures with a puzzle, or unanswered question.
ALARM threatens with immediate consequences.
PRESTIGE earns respect through symbols of achievement.
POWER is command over others.
VICE tempts with "forbidden fruit," causing us to step outside our usual habits or behaviors.
TRUST comforts us with certainty and reliability.

In Parts I and II of this book, we saw how fascination already shapes our actions and opinions in surprising ways. An effective fascination plan harnesses this power. Once you understand the triggers that drive your customers' behavior, and design your plan with your triggers and badges in mind, you can direct this force of attraction. Are you using the right triggers, in the right way, to get your desired result?

Your Brand's Chemistry Set

Let's take a few well-known brands, and check out how their current branding successfully activates specific triggers. (There's some degree of subjectivity involved with this exercise, so expect and enjoy healthy debate. The point is to identify and establish patterns.)

The Appeal of Lust + Trust for Mass Brands

We don't necessarily think of Coke, Olive Garden, and Rachael Ray as similar brands. However, they all rely on the same two triggers as many mainstream food-oriented brands: lust and trust. (Many Kraft products have almost exactly the same formula as Olive Garden.)

Each brand uses different secondary triggers, in addition to lust and trust. For instance, we saw how Coke amps up mystique, through mythology. Olive Garden adds a bit of the alarm trigger with notorious wait times for a table, and time-limited specials. And Rachael Ray gives a splash of vice when she encourages viewers to tweak recipes as they go, or when she sneaks in extra "delish" bites.

Trend-Oriented Brands

In contrast to the lust + trust combination, brands that tap into trends tend to trade on other triggers, without emphasis on the consistency and safety of trust.

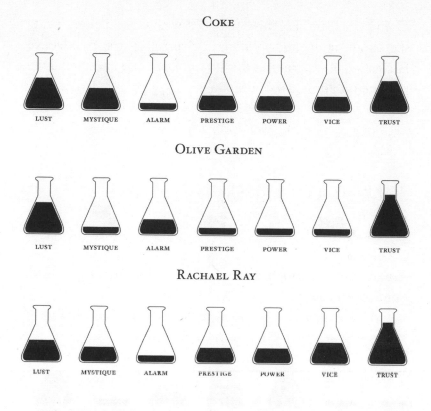

COKE

LUST · MYSTIQUE · ALARM · PRESTIGE · POWER · VICE · TRUST

OLIVE GARDEN

LUST · MYSTIQUE · ALARM · PRESTIGE · POWER · VICE · TRUST

RACHAEL RAY

LUST · MYSTIQUE · ALARM · PRESTIGE · POWER · VICE · TRUST

The chain of W Hotels (part of Starwood Hotels & Resorts) tempts urban travelers with all manner of saucy treats. One offer is a "Seduce Me" package: When you "sneak away for a racy rendezvous" they'll provide not only a bottle of bubbly and late checkout, but in addition, their "pleasurable playthings are sure to spice up your escape."

Have you ever been inside a Sephora? This sophisticated cosmetics and beauty store not only allows consumers to sample products, but spurs them on to experience and experiment with all the trendiest fragrances, imported creams, and shimmering makeups. Sephora lives in a different category from W Hotels, but their triggers mirror each other, and they share a similar a message: Indulge,

W Hotels

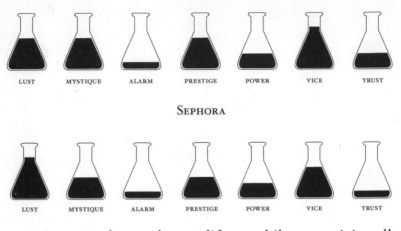

LUST   MYSTIQUE   ALARM   PRESTIGE   POWER   VICE   TRUST

Sephora

LUST   MYSTIQUE   ALARM   PRESTIGE   POWER   VICE   TRUST

experiment, and upgrade your life . . . while never giving all your secrets away.

FedEx

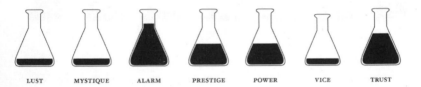

LUST   MYSTIQUE   ALARM   PRESTIGE   POWER   VICE   TRUST

Who's Getting It Right (Or Not)?

Federal Express thrives on triggering alarm. When the threat of negative consequences runs high, we're willing to pay extra for overnight service in order to trust that it will arrive.

The Walt Disney World experience is based upon stories, and stories form a foundation of mystique. In addition, visitors know they'll step inside a highly sensory environment. And for many of us, Disney World fulfills a trusted expectation: Our children will enjoy something similar to our own first Disney experiences years ago.

WALT DISNEY WORLD THEME PARK

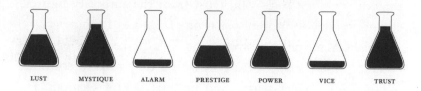

| LUST | MYSTIQUE | ALARM | PRESTIGE | POWER | VICE | TRUST |

Who's *not* triggering much of anything? Kmart offers very little in the way of fascination. The brand has some of the trust trigger from name recognition. They sometimes use the alarm trigger for sales: remember "Attention Kmart Shoppers!" and "Blue Light Specials"? There is also the stockholder's alarm, during the filing of Chapter 11 in 2002. Other than that, Kmart is not living up to Target's fearsome fascination combo of lust (with its brilliantly iconic marketing and design), prestige (bringing high style to the masses), vice (for instance, consumers can find reasonably priced versions of designer clothes), and trust (with the brand's consistently good taste), as well as a bucketful of lust (and it's a bucket designed by Philippe Starck or Michael Graves).

KMART

| LUST | MYSTIQUE | ALARM | PRESTIGE | POWER | VICE | TRUST |

Archetypes and Superheroes

The seven triggers apply to every type of message and personality, and even to archetypical comic book superheroes.

We may never get to see Superman and Spider-Man battle it out in real life, but we *can* see how these two superheroes' triggers stack up. Superman, the quintessential all-American superhero, fascinates us with dashing good looks, meteor-exploding ability, rock-solid trust from the authority figures, and occasional kryptonite poisoning from Lex Luthor.

Spider-Man, on the other hand, is a darker alter ego. He evokes a different set of triggers with a fully masked costume, web-slingers, "spider-sense," and nemesis Doctor Octopus. He doesn't always follow authority and has been arrested (far different from mild-mannered Clark Kent!). This intriguing combo has generated enough mystique and vice to spellbind us since 1962.

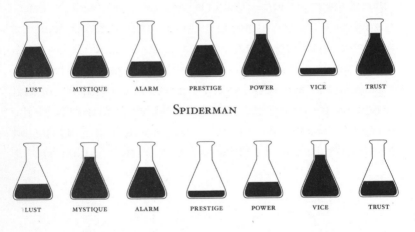

SUPERMAN

LUST   MYSTIQUE   ALARM   PRESTIGE   POWER   VICE   TRUST

SPIDERMAN

LUST   MYSTIQUE   ALARM   PRESTIGE   POWER   VICE   TRUST

Exercise: Your Brand's "Chemistry Set"

Imagine seven beakers on the table in front of you. Each beaker has a label: lust, mystique, alarm, prestige, power, vice, and trust. Some beakers are close to empty, some are half full, and if you're lucky, one is filled near the top. These seven elements combine in a sort of chemical formula, a.k.a your brand.

These seven potential fascination triggers offer an infinite number of brand combinations. You can blend or separate them, dial them up or pull them back. You can reinvigorate your whole

identity by adding or subtracting small amounts of a single trigger, or revise your ratios depending on your goals. The point will
be to develop the most irresistible recipe, and make it your own.
Your "chemical formula" may also use secondary triggers, ones
used less frequently or to a lesser degree.

On a piece of paper or whiteboard, draw the seven beakers,
one for each trigger. Now estimate your current levels of fascination: How full is each beaker? Which beakers should be more
full, or less full, in order to fulfill your goals? Keep these levels
in mind as we move forward into Stage 2, so you can calibrate
according to your badges, and your bell curve.

Okay, now you've evaluated your message. How might you
use the seven triggers to develop it?

Stage 2: Development

Create and Heighten Fascination

By now we have an idea of how you generate fascination—and how much of it you generate. The next stage is my favorite part of the whole process: Develop new ways to fascinate others. Time to put creativity to work for us.

Fascination Badges

No matter what type of brand you are, no matter what type of message you spread, you already have raw ingredients to be fascinating. I call these ingredients "fascination badges" because they're emblematic of what you represent. So how, exactly, are you fascinating? Seven potential areas:

1. Purpose: Your reason for being; your function as a brand.

2. Core beliefs: The code of values and principles that guide you; what you stand for.

3. Heritage: Your reputation and history; the "backstory" of how you came to be.

4. Products: The goods, services, or information you produce.

5. Benefits: The promises of reward for purchasing the product, both tangible and abstract, overt and implied.

6. Actions: How you conduct yourself.

7. Culture: All the characteristics of your identity, including personality, executional style, and mind-set.

Badges allow employees, customers, and fans to identify themselves with you, and through you, beyond product usage. They invite people inside your brand, allowing them to participate and take ownership. Find them,* and then methodically refine and expand them.

---

* Examples of where to uncover your badges:

Culture: Make a list of unorthodox customs, unusual traits, or quirky habits within your company itself. Even the smallest traditions can reveal deeper values, showcasing your brand's uniquely fascinating point of view. How do you prepare for a launch, or celebrate your success? Are there policies or processes that represent your perspective? Ad agency Crispin Porter + Bogusky's employee manual (really more of a culture manual) is available to all for download.

Heritage: Examine your own heritage. What patterns continually emerge? What watershed decisions shaped your ethos? What people or products exemplify your DNA? Browse the attic of your past. Find things from your history that were fascinating at one time, but failed to hold interest. (Remember Colt 45 and their newly hip brown bags?)

Intangible assets: Do you have unexploited intellectual property hiding in the corners? Below-the-radar accomplishments? Talents that rarely see the light of day? Relationships that could become fascinating partnerships? Inactive licenses? How about unused R&D, such as sidelined innovations or research without analysis?

Exercise: Create New Badges

One by one, go through the seven types of badges, and brainstorm every possible association for each. Starting with your "purpose," for example, list all the words, ideas, and associations, gleaned from every possible source, from your mission statement to your implied intentions. The more specific, the better. Next, move on to core beliefs. And so on. What patterns emerge? A few real-life badges to get you started:

• **Heritage:** At Nike, business cards feature a drawing of a waffle iron, commemorating the "aha" moment when founder Bill Bowerman poured rubber into his wife's waffle iron, thereby creating Nike's original racer sole design.

• **Core beliefs:** The Martin Agency, famous for its inclusive culture, designed its new building with a circular foyer two stories high. The foyer is aesthetically beautiful, but also serves as a literal representation of the company's core values: At company meetings, every employee can be part of the discussion.

• **Culture:** Fascination badges started long before formal marketing in the twentieth century. In the seventeenth century, carrots were either purple or red. But then the Dutch royal family, named the House of Orange, needed a "brand campaign" to exemplify their powerful influence. They could have sewn a bigger flag, or painted a fancier crest, or trained a fiercer army. Instead, horticulturists created a way to turn the country's favorite vegetable, the carrot, into a symbol of the national color. As you've seen for yourself, carrots have been carroty orange ever since.

Badges and Bell Curves

You just brainstormed all your badges in seven categories, and even created new ones. Now we're going to find which ones are fascinating—or could *become* fascinating.

Imagine a bell curve for the "purpose" badge list you brainstormed above. On this bell curve, you'd plot unremarkable product associations at the left, moderately interesting ones in the middle, and extraordinary ones at the far right. Many of your purpose badges will collect in the middle (because they're not meeting the Gold Hallmarks for a fascinating message). However, you might have a purpose that goes way out at the edge . . . an outlier.

Malcolm Gladwell, author of the book *Outliers*, says that "outlier" is "a scientific term to describe things or phenomena that lie outside normal experience." Your goal is to find or create your own "outliers," badges that are an extreme deviation from the mean. These meet criteria from our list of Gold Hallmarks, and as a result, fascinate people in the extreme. If you can find an outlier that's three standard deviations away from the center, you're on to something.

Exercise: Finding the Edge of Your Bell Curve

This exercise draws upon everything we've done so far in this section: badges, hallmarks, and bell curve, as well as your seven fascination trigger options. The steps:

1. List your badges (both existing and potential).
2. Evaluate against the hallmarks of a fascinating brand.
3. Plot on a bell curve.
4. Push badges outward on the curve by infusing them with more of your primary trigger.
5. Push badges outward on the curve by infusing them with a new trigger.
6. Build your message around these badges.

Draw a bell curve, and take all the aspects of a single badge that you brainstormed above, and plot them on the curve.

For the sake of discussion, let's pick the "heritage" badge. Your heritage might be inherently fascinating, or it might not. If not, either go on to your next badge, or better yet, stop and find ways to make your heritage more fascinating. A furniture company with an eighteenth-century legacy or noteworthy story behind the founder could have an outlier, because those badges would score highly on the hallmarks. A software company that launched only yesterday might not have strong heritage badges. But how might this startup turn its lack of heritage into a fascination badge? To increase the fascination level of a badge, apply more of your triggers.

Now go on to your next badge category. Repeat.

Ask Yourself:

- What could happen if you took an uninteresting badge and pushed it a little further, and a little further, to see how far you can go? Sears introduced a "products" badge: the first replacement guarantee of its kind, for any tool bearing the Craftsman name. This new guarantee wasn't one year or ten years as other competitors offered; it was a *lifetime* replacement guarantee, reaching out to the edge of the bell curve and becoming a powerful trust badge. Sears was willing to go all the way to the edge, where no one in the category had gone.

The Fringe

The degree to which you are willing to step outside your category norms is the degree to which you'll fascinate others.

The Ritz-Carlton hotel chain is an outlier in customer service.

While it's not a formally acknowledged policy, any Ritz-Carlton employee is reportedly permitted to spend up to $2,000 to ensure that a guest's problem is immediately handled. (That's prestige partnered tightly with trust, to ensure credibility.) The more unchallenged a norm appears to be, the more fascination you can earn by tweaking it.

Celebrity nightclubs live at the fringe. Otherwise, a hotspot becomes a "coldspot." In Las Vegas, Rum Jungle advertises a cocktail for $8,200, with Rémy Martin Louis XIII cognac and Roederer Cristal Champagne, served "on the rocks." The rocks? A pair of 1.5-carat diamond earrings. (That's the prestige trigger, mixed liberally with vice and lust.)

If Cristal isn't your thing, try Hooters. The chain restaurant, whose tagline is "Delightfully tacky, yet unrefined," offers a meal package with twenty chicken wings and a bottle of Dom Pérignon. (That's the prestige trigger combined with, um . . . orange Dolphin shorts in size XS and tan pantyhose.)

Fringes Have No Boundaries

In the safe confines of the creative process, explore as far as you can into the fringe wilderness. When you're ready to launch your message in the market, you might not push your message to the maximum intensity—in many cases, that'd be overwhelming, even a turnoff. But at this point of development, don't be afraid to raise the stakes. Better to be exceptional in one or two areas than pretty good in all.

Exercise: Identify Outliers of Your Fringe

Remember the chemistry set? Now that you know your main trigger, how far can you push it? If your trigger is prestige, how can you embody that in the extreme? In this exercise, the goal is to see just how far you might extend to the outermost tip of the bell curve.

Here, you'll find prime fascination territory. The more extraordinary your badges, the more fascinating they can become. As you're expanding possibilities, push past the obvious. Past what you've done before. Past what your competition is doing. Keep going. No, a little further. (C'mon, there's good stuff in there, but you have to go out and find it!) At the fringe, you'll develop your most highly concentrated badges.

Say you're a leading diaper brand. You make perfectly good diapers, ones that absorb without leaks, and have comfy Velcro on the sides. Your product benefits are necessary; however, as badges, they're not fascinating. These badges plop in the middle of your bell curve, rather than out at the fringe. How might you create fascinating badges? If you created a line of diaper covers with Gwen Stefani's LAMB fashion label, that would activate prestige (the trigger) and get people talking (the hallmark). There's your badge. If you made fully flushable diaper for eco-tourists, you'd activate trust (the trigger), and become part of a social revolution (the hallmark). If the diaper's exterior were printed with a simple visual story, the ending of which was hidden in invisible ink until your child wet the diaper, that would pique the curiosity of mystique (the trigger), as well as prompt positive and not-so-positive strong and immediate reactions (the hallmark).

Ask Yourself:

- What happens if you step your toe over the line, and revise an accepted norm? Identify how you could start to offer one truly inimitable difference.
- How could you redefine a specific expectation, as Ritz-Carlton has done? You've hit the jackpot if you can get people to start conversations about your brand with the phrase, "Wow, cool, I can't believe what Company X just did for me . . ."

Incorporating a New Trigger

A trigger that might seem unsuitable by itself can perfectly accent another trigger. Together, the two triggers build a more compelling overall message.

If your primary fascination element is *prestige*, should you consider *alarm*? If your primary fascination element is *lust*, how might you ramp up your *power*? Under what circumstances should you leverage another trigger entirely?

At certain growth stages, a trigger that was once fascinating can become a weakness. This might be because your audience changed, or your category evolved, or technology leaped ahead; in any case, triggers are a means to an end and must change accordingly. As we saw, Harry Winston relied upon prestige for decades, but when new competitors emerged and the category shifted, the brand incorporated power.

Club Med faced a similar need for change. The brand's former tagline neatly summed up a generational wild streak: "The antidote to civilization." For years, Club Med was the place to rid yourself of civilization's many irritating conventions (moderation, marital vows, et al.). The tagline itself reeked of vice. But as the political climate was swinging to the right, Club Med fell out of sync and stopped its swinging. It refocused where the money was: parents and families, adopting prestige (attracting a laid-back international coterie) and lust (cuisine, scenery, spa treatments). Club Med's transition is successfully complete.* Other examples when you might want to dial up, or dial down, new triggers:

If your trigger is *trust*, you're building a reputation upon consistency. Yet trust can eventually begin to feel ho-hum

---

* I imagine Club Med must have been quite an interesting vacation as it transitioned its occupancy list from semi-naked hedonists to suburban families. "Sir, I'm sorry, you'll have to put your bathing suit on while at the breakfast table."

and predictable. What if you laced a little *alarm* into the mix? You'd increase urgency and action around your message, and add just enough adrenaline to keep things interesting.

If you increase a bit of *lust*, you'll encourage people to step in more closely and participate.

If you currently trigger *prestige*, you're elevating your status and rank. Yet be careful not to become so aloof and unattainable that your target feels uncomfortable with your message.

Mystique will make people want to ask questions, learn more, and share what they know. That curiosity keeps it from feeling cliché or status-conscious.

Additionally, *prestige* brands must take care in releasing new communication, since tossing out random information can cloud your message or fail to meet expectations. Again, mystique can strengthen prestige here as well, allowing you to withhold information and release only the minimum necessary.

Is *power* your thing? The power trigger is a favorite with corporations, because it establishes leadership. Yet messages with power run the risk of feeling corporate and self-inflated, or worse, steely and detached. To avoid intimidating your audience, add just a drop or two of *lust* for warmth and approachability in your message.

If your message is feeling stale or ponderous, consider a whit of *vice*, which encourages your audience to consider new alternative ways of thinking and behaving. This zesty little trigger helps people experience your message anew, rather than taking it for granted as the "same old, same old."

Exercise: Combine Your Primary Trigger with a New One

One of my clients, Cole Haan, had a legacy of the prestige trigger. Everyone knows the products are well crafted, but they lacked the level of lust normally reserved for trendier prestige brands such as Gucci and Jimmy Choo. To fight back, Cole Haan tapped new technology from parent company Nike, engineering a new design of cushioned four-inch high-heeled shoes. With this invention, high heels weren't just for Town Car–cruising socialites and masochists. Women who do crazy things like *walk* could now wear shoes with both prestige and lust. One appearance on *Oprah* later, and early designs were sold out across the country.

Ask Yourself:

- Go through the list of seven triggers. For each one, consider a possibility for how you might incorporate it with your primary trigger. You might be surprised.

Cautionary Tale: Use Care When Switching Triggers

If you choose to alter your trigger, that's fine, but stick to your core values unless you're ready for a massive overhaul. Even if you piggyback on trends, don't violate your core values. Celebrity chef Wolfgang Puck's company scores high on lust (craveable foods), and prestige (trendy restaurants such as Spago). By releasing supermarket soups and airport pizzas, he retains the core values of his brand for a broader market.

When customers buy a product, what they're often actually buying is something more than the utility of the item—they're buying a trigger. If they pay for your product, but you don't deliver the expected trigger, you could face a backlash. Here's an example. If a consumer expects to buy the trust trigger, but instead gets the vice trigger, it violates expectations. Kelly Clarkson made one such faux pas. When Clarkson became the first *American Idol* winner, her fans' expectations were clearly defined: She was the newly christened American pop princess, bubble gum and sparkles. But then Clarkson threw the world a curveball with her third album, *My December.* The new darker, grittier Clarkson broke her core values (trust trigger). Songs such as "Haunted" and "Sober" were deemed "too negative" by her own label. Failing to fascinate fans, Clarkson canceled her tour due to underwhelming ticket sales, and sought new management. Madonna, on the other hand, reinvents by the day; reinvention is a core value of hers.

It's good and necessary to evolve your message over time. However, changing your trigger entirely and without warning might just end up creating the alarm trigger for your accountants.

What If . . . ?

Okay! This is where the brainstorming really kicks in. "What if" questions sit at the heart of any fascination development process, allowing us to apply everything we've established in the exercises so far. *What if* you ramped up your primary trigger? *What if* you incorporated a new trigger? *What if* you went 180 degrees in the other direction of your category's expected triggers? This type of exploration should continue indefinitely, but in the interest of helping you imagine the possibilities, I'll demonstrate how I unfurl the process with clients.

EXAMPLE 1: A SINGLE TRIGGER, A SINGLE PRODUCT, APPLIED IN MULTIPLE WAYS

What If You Applied the Prestige Trigger to an Unprestigious Item?

PRESTIGE AND THE T-SHIRT

Prestige, as you'll recall, is why we fixate on symbols of rank and respect. Items of prestige have cultural meaning because they communicate a group's priorities and values. How could a mass-market product, such as a T-shirt, trigger prestige? Obviously you could sew a designer logo or emboss it with rhinestones, sure. But what if . . .

· WHAT IF YOU MADE THE T-SHIRT SCARCE?

Create T-shirt designs by famous artists that are available only in limited editions of ten thousand. Or editions of one hundred. Or editions of one. When an edition is sold out, it's gone forever (or at least until it pops up—ding!—on eBay).

· WHAT IF YOU TURNED THE T-SHIRT'S PURCHASE INTO A PRESTIGIOUS EXPERIENCE?

Design a high-end "mobile T-shirt boutique" that visits customers at bachelorette parties or baby showers. Bring consumers a carefully curated selection of T-shirts, thereby increasing their perceived value.

· WHAT IF YOU MADE IT FROM CULTURALLY SIGNIFICANT MATERIALS?

Make the shirt from a fabric that holds special appeal. Sew it from distressed concert T-shirts, or UK football jerseys.

· WHAT IF YOU MADE IT FEEL CUSTOMIZED?

Allow customers to customize their T-shirt design (lettering, color, embroidery, etc.) and then watch online, in real time, via streaming video, as their T-shirt is made in the workshop. By the time the shirt arrives, customers already have an attachment to their shirt.

· WHAT IF PEOPLE HAD TO EARN THE T-SHIRT?

Make consumers "pay" for your T-shirt, above and beyond the price tag. (My nephew has a T-shirt from Cancun that announces his tequila prowess: "I ate the worm!" Now, admittedly, that might not be my personal idea of fascinating prestige, but it is for his target audience.)

▪ WHAT IF YOU MADE THE T-SHIRT TOO EXPENSIVE NOT JUST FOR MOST CONSUMERS, BUT FOR ALMOST ALL CONSUMERS?

How can you make the ubiquitous white T-shirt less ubiquitous? Chanel makes a $500 T-shirt; Prada, a $1,500 one. Both have sold fairly briskly. Who says you can't make a $15,000 T-shirt? You might never, ever sell a single one. And that's not the point. You'd provoke conversations.

▪ WHAT IF YOU TAPPED INTO DEEPER VALUES?

People pay more for brands whose beliefs connect with their own. What if your T-shirts were woven from recycled hemp? What if you started a "T-shirt relief" program that employed families in global disaster zones, building free housing in exchange for their skills, and donors get T-shirts? Or what if you created the world's first "LEED certified" T-shirts?

Now apply this logic to yourself and your brand. What would compel your customer to associate prestige with *you*?

EXAMPLE 2: A SINGLE COMPANY, MULTIPLE TRIGGERS

The truth is, marketers can get into ruts. Our television commercials can get into ruts: We rely on winding roads to sell cars, cute animals to sell toilet paper, and ethnically nondescript families sitting around a dinner table to sell spaghetti sauce. We also get into ruts with triggers: We use prestige to sell expensive items, vice to sell energy drinks, and lust to sell perfume. It's all a bit trite, really. Sometimes it's important to play against type, and apply unexpected triggers. In this "what if" example, we'll apply unexpected triggers to a single small company, staying away from the clichés.

JUDGING A BOOK BY ITS TRIGGERS

What If You Activated New Triggers Within a Traditional Category?

Let's say you're marketing a small neighborhood bookshop. Obviously, you'll be competing against a massive market leader: Amazon.

com. How could you convince people to go out of their way to visit your store, pay higher prices, and forgo services such as automatic billing? By applying the triggers, of course.

• WHAT IF YOU TRIGGERED TRUST?

Could you trigger it relatively quickly, through a frequent-buyer program? Or trigger it more intensively, by interacting with every customer on a first-name basis.

• WHAT IF YOU TRIGGERED LUST?

Your small bookshop could offer an intimate fireplace, or ergonomic reading chairs.

• WHAT IF YOU TRIGGERED ALARM?

Alarm uses consequences or a deadline to prompt fast action. You might carry a hard-to-find book, and stock just ten of them, giving customers a reason to shop immediately.

• WHAT IF YOU TRIGGERED MYSTIQUE?

Change your stock once a week, each week with a different theme, and always a surprise. One week, you might line the shelves with books about the ocean (from marine biology to *Old Man and the Sea*), and the next you might delight consumers with a monkey-related theme (*Planet of the Apes*, *Tarzan*, and *Curious George*).

• WHAT IF YOU TRIGGERED POWER?

Power controls the environment. A bookstore could develop its own unique system of evaluating books: for example, a "favorites" selection in the spirit of Jack Covert and Todd Sattersten's *The 100 Best Business Books of All Time*.

• WHAT IF YOU TRIGGERED VICE?

Vice entices people away from their routine behavior. Encourage customers to take one day a year to turn off the computer, stay home from work, and read their favorite new books . . . purchased from your shop, of course.

WHAT IF YOU TRIGGERED PRESTIGE?

Exclusively carry first editions and autographed copies. Or make your entire store accessible to a membership-only cadre.

IN STAGES 1 AND 2, we've been living in the world of possibility: thinking of what you *might* do or *could* do. Now let's talk about what you actually *will* do. Time to bring all this conceptual goodness into execution.

Stage 3: Execution

Bringing Your Fascination to Life

B y this point, you've established your current scenario, and you've developed new ideas. Now we'll bring to life all the strategies and ideas we've developed so far. When I work with clients, this stage becomes extremely customized because each industry has its own nuances, as does each company and product, fluctuating with the industry, all driven by the brand personality. Stage 3 won't outline exercises, because by this point, your Plan of Attack will be different from anyone else's, and will depend entirely upon your context (because as we now know, ideas are only precious in a specific context). Yet short of working together in person, let's continue with your Plan of Attack. There isn't one defined approach, but there *are* defined principles.

Before you unleash your new plan with your main audience, you must first consider how you will help it become fascinating *within your own group*.

Building Internal Support for Your Fascination Plan

You now have a clearer understanding of where you're connecting with your audience, and where black holes lurk. You have a range of potential badges, and a bell curve for making your existing ideas more fascinating. But that's not enough. You also need your team's full support.

Every message needs advocates in order to survive. When presenting ideas, as is always the case, fascination isn't measured in what you say, but in what others say *about you*.

Sharing Your Fascination Plan with Others

It's one thing to come up with new ideas, but quite another to create advocates from your partners, clients, investors, board of directors, or anyone else holding the mighty approval stamp. At first, fascinating ideas can feel risky, so managing this process wisely takes extra thought.

- *In the face of increased risk, you must increase evidence and payoff.* The more unorthodox the idea, the more evidence you'll need to sell it, and the greater the payoff must be to justify it.

- *Build the most rational possible argument.* Don't try to sell a new idea with abstractions like "word of mouth." Early in the process, substantiate your idea with potential timelines, anticipated costs, and partners. Remove as many variables and unknowns as possible, to demonstrate control. Hypothetical is okay at this stage, but be as specific as possible.

- *Show how you've succeeded in a parallel situation.* Back up your ideas with reference points or comparable case studies. If you haven't accumulated this success track record yet, show how concepts such as the one you've proposed have masterfully succeeded in the past.

- *Help your client or boss "sell up."* If someone else will be defending your idea to higher levels, make sure that person has the understanding and tools to do so. Once you've made sure that the presenter can clearly articulate the idea, then make sure that the presentation itself can stand on its own, without you there.

In the preface, we learned that for thousands of years, everyone from academics to ordinary folk viewed fascination as witchcraft. Hopefully by now we agree that fascination isn't witchcraft, and can be measured, researched, and reevaluated.

Measure, Research, Reevaluate

If you're a marketer, odds are you've already done the research on your customers: You know who they are, where they are, and what they're buying. You might have gigabytes of information, an R&D department full of facts, or even a hardbound deck of McKinsey & Company analysis. What you probably lack, despite all these data, is an understanding of how to change the nature of your relationship with consumers by becoming more fascinating.

Without the benefit of knowing your scenario and goals, we'll keep this big-picture. The following points will help chart the course of refining your Plan of Attack.

Moving Beyond Traditional Research

In your market research, are you asking the right questions, and looking in the right places, to measure fascination? It's not always a simple matter. While it's relatively easy to measure awareness and recall, fascination is trickier. It's intangible and subjective, often defying logic and analysis. Unlike measurements such as "share of voice," we can't easily calculate fascination metrics such as "share of attraction" or "share of mystique." However, we do have guidelines: our Gold Hallmarks of a Fascinating Message, and your F Score. As you consider these, also keep two points in mind.

Two Points to Remember

- Don't just track the message *you* create. Instead, track the ways in which your message inspires others to create messages *about you*.
- The effectiveness of your message is measured not by how many people hear that message or even remember it, but by how many *listen* to it, *talk about* it with other people, and, ultimately, *take action* on it.

Traditional analysis works well for traditional messages. But with fascination, you'll need to slightly alter the ways in which you follow through. Start by reconsidering a few basic points.

- *Reconsider your goals.* Traditional marketing had generalized goals, such as increased sales and greater loyalty. But in today's fragmented ADD world, those are way too general. Your plan will benefit from more specific goals, and fascination can help. Do you want to increase foot traffic in your retail locations by pulling people into your stores to interact with your products (as Apple and Sephora do with lust)? The more specific your goals, the more accurately you can reach them.

- *Reconsider your metrics.* What metric will be most useful for your overall goals? Measuring "awareness" of your message is good, and standard practice, yet by itself, awareness is too passive and limited. Go beyond traditional means of evaluating a consumer's degree of connection to reveal factors such as number of mentions in mainstream media, satisfaction index, and percentage of increase in social media mentions.

Track Your Progress

Traditionally, tracking a company's marketing success would revolve around the number of products sold or services hired. But by following a number of indicators, you can more tangibly and specifically measure your increase in fascination.*

Removing Barriers to Fascination

Companies that fascinate audiences over the long term share certain qualities. Evaluation, development, and execution of

---

* Examples of ways to measure fascination:

Community participation in your online media: Includes number of members / subscribers joined, download counts, RSS subscriptions, page views, length of visit, number of comments, trackbacks, and posts on other blogs. Number of customer complaints, suggestions, and questions. YouTube traffic, MySpace members, Facebook pages, category chat forums and wikis.

Content creation and distribution about your brand by outside (unpaid) parties: Includes mentions in prominent blogs, social networks, and mainstream media, as well as user-generated content (YouTube uploads, Podcasts, Vodcasts, Twitter). Track what your audience is *saying* about your brand with Google Alerts, Technorati, Digg, Techmeme, Stumbleupon, and del.i.cious. Measure what your audience is *doing* around your brand through Google Analytics, Feedburner, and Technorati.

Offline participation: Tracking fascination in the offline world requires a more finely tuned ear to the ground. List every location and touchpoint where a potential customer could encounter the product, benefits, and media you produce. Note other forms of increased energy around your brand: business inquiries and sales leads, interview requests and spontaneous referrals, fan clubs about your brand, and third-party branded merchandise (drinking cups with your logo, T-shirts, bumper stickers, etc.).

fascinating ideas should be a collective goal, one with resources and support from the C suite all the way through the ranks.

- *Slaughter the sacred cow.* What policies and practices do we have in place only because "that's the way it's always been done"? What corporate or marketing dogma is so "sacred" within your company that it seems off-limits to questioning? And how can you start questioning it?

- *Awaken sleepy traditions.* What might have been fascinating at one time can soon become unremarkable. Crayola's first contest to name a color, in 1993, drew two million entries. But without changing the format, participation has dwindled to a measly twenty-five thousand entries. How can you update the same-old, same-old?

- *Raise the stakes.* What would you do if your company's life depended upon earning fascination in the next year? In the next month? In the next twenty-four hours? Now?

- *Avoid committee mentality.* The most fascinating ideas are often fragile because they can be easily "dumbed down." (Who's your Chief Fascination Officer?)

- *Earn trust.* Trust, as we know, is confidence based on prior experience. In an ADD world, preferences and ideas and relationships change constantly, but trust remains. Prestige and mystique are great triggers to have, but your most fascinating asset will be your ability to continually earn trust from peers, the press, and the community.

Still Fascination-Resistant? Questions for Your Team to Consider

- What policies and protocol block fascination by forcing a "red tape" mentality, or an overthought, overcontrolled approval process?

- Is there a percentage of revenue that you can stake on fascination-oriented projects?

- What offerings within the company are a commodity or parity? How can you tweak those, even slightly, to become unique enough to generate interest?

- Is the group so concerned with neutrality that your communication is diluted down to gray mush? Are you so focused on keeping a low profile, playing it safe, that you're killing fascination opportunities before they've had a chance to hatch? (Fascination requires putting yourself out there for remarkable ideas, accomplishments, and innovations.)

- Are you trying to keep too tight a grip on fascination? You can't keep fascination private from your own audience. The moment you try to own it, you risk killing it.

By applying the seven triggers to a product or message, and by measuring results against the Gold Hallmarks, a company can consistently engage consumers, carving out a niche that cannot be filled by anyone or anything else. But before any of this branding goodness can happen, the company must first develop a culture of fascination within its own organization. For some groups, this requires a significant shift. If the purpose of fascination is to help people connect, then we must first support an environment of connecting with each other in the workplace, so our most fascinating ideas survive and flourish.

You'll find out how fascination affects behavior in the workplace in our appendix, "The Kelton Fascination Study." You'll also discover whether people will spend more for fascinating products (hint: yes), as well as the amount people will pay to become more fascinating to others (hint: it's more than you think).

Appendix:
The Kelton Fascination Study

Women will spend more to be fascinating than they spend on food. In fact, women will spend more to be fascinating then they spend on food and clothes combined.

They will pay an average of $338 per month to become the most fascinating person in the room, roughly 15 percent of their net income. This finding was on page 46 of the Kelton Fascination Study, conducted by national public opinion company Kelton Research. Developed for this book, the study surveyed 1,059 Americans around the country, ages eighteen and over.[*]

To our knowledge, there's never been an in-depth national survey on this topic. The survey included a lengthy list of questions on the relationship between fascination and decision

---

[*] Kelton Research is a global public opinion company. It works with more than thirty of the Fortune 100 corporations, including McDonald's, Target, and Pepsi. Twice it has been named "fastest-growing market research consultancy" by *Inc.* magazine, and in 2008, *Entrepreneur* named it to its Hot 100 Companies list.

making: brand choices, careers, relationships, and personal self-image. Our goal was to define the role of fascination in people's lives, measure it in tangible terms, and learn more about general themes.

- How much is fascination actually worth, in dollar amounts?
- Are people willing to pay more for fascinating products?
- In what ways do people differ in their levels of fascination (men versus women, CEOs versus college students, New Yorkers versus people in the Midwest)?
- What exactly determines if a message, or product, is fascinating?
- What behaviors do people exhibit when fascinated?

The resulting research offers a breadth and depth of insight.[*] (Some answers surprised us, some didn't.) But the numbers reveal more. The numbers tell us the role of fascination in people's vanities and insecurities, love lives and work lives, secret obsessions and public personae. It doesn't take much analysis to see the respondents' frustrations at work, and their inviolable connection to their children. As a whole, it's not just a study about fascination, but a look at how people feel about themselves and their lives in general.

Topline Findings

- *People will pay a great deal of money if you can help them become fascinating.* On average they will pay $288/month

---

[*] The results of the study fill a four-inch-thick binder, which I don't recommend reviewing without reading glasses due to its exceedingly small type.

to be the most fascinating person in a room. (Five percent will pay more than $1,000/month.) In addition to paying more, they'll invest more energy in you and your product.

- *People will pay a great deal of money if you can help them feel fascinated.* A fascinating brand can charge more than an unfascinating one. People also will pay a premium for brands that activate desired triggers. In the presence of a fascinating product, people report a physical, intellectual, and emotional response, and sometimes even an "adrenaline rush."

- *People will go to surprising lengths to have a more fascinating life.* They want to feel more engaged and immersed. And not only will they pay to be fascinated, but when asked how far they would go for a fascinating life, six out of ten people said they would bend their morals, standards, or loyalties. Among unmarried people, that number rises to seven out of ten.

The Role of Fascination in Personal and Marketing Messages
How Can Fascination Shape Decision Making?

- *If you want to measure whether you're fascinating someone . . .* When fascinated by a product, 80 percent report behaving differently: doing research, talking to friends, protecting it, touching it, or even reporting a physical response when in contact with the item of their fascination. (If you're a marketer, track tangible behaviors to know whether your product is effectively fascinating consumers.)

- *If you're interested in communicating to a younger audience . . .* Younger consumers are more interested in being *fascinating* than *fascinated.* (By giving them opportunities to captivate others, you open the door to higher sales and/or price point for your brand.)

- *If you're thinking about abandoning the personal touch . . .* While the digital space offers endlessly unique experiences, 81 percent of us have most fascinating conversations in person rather than online. In-person contact is still the most compelling and can drive deeper relationships.

- *If you're thinking about hiring a celebrity spokesperson . . .* We think of celebrities as fascinating; however, 78 percent of Americans are more fascinated with the lives of their families. (Yet as we'll see below, they're still bored by their own lives.)

- *If you're wondering about customizing your message for different parts of the country . . .* People respond differently, based on their geography. Lust is more fascinating on the West Coast. Trust is most fascinating in the Midwest. And in the Northeast, it's about power. (Those lucky Northeasterners also report having more fascinating lives than anyone else in the country.)

- *If you want to align yourself with something that's already fascinating . . .* By a landslide, the most fascinating entity in people's lives is their own children. An overwhelming 96 percent of parents find their own children fascinating.

- *If you want to tap into groups that are already fascinated . . .*
  Groups most likely to report feeling fascinated by their
  own lives: parents, married people, women, people ages
  eighteen to thirty-nine, those who earn more than
  $50,000 per year, and those with a hobby.

- *If you're still wondering if fascination matters for marketers . . .*
  People will pay up to three times as much for a product or
  experience that they find "intensely captivating."

The Kelton Study at Work
Fascinating Your Bosses, Employees, Co-Workers, and Clients
Fascinated employees are more engaged with their work, and
more loyal to their bosses and companies. Still, there's no such
thing as one-size-fits-all fascination.

- *Who is most fascinated by work? Those at the beginning
  of their careers, and those at the peak of success.* Those in
  their twenties are highly fascinated by their careers, as are
  CEOs and senior managers.

- *Married employees are also likely to be "extremely fascinated
  at work."* Maybe married employees have a greater ap-
  preciation for stability. Or maybe the singles scene makes
  work seem less interesting by comparison?

- *A fascinating personal life is three times more important
  than a fascinating work life.* Another reason companies
  should support a healthy work/life balance. (Perhaps
  giving employees a day off with family is more important
  than that office holiday party.)

- *We're at our peak of fascination with work while in our forties.* This group says they become the most engrossed in their work, compared to the rest of the population. Of these, 55 percent are fascinated at least once a day and sometimes more. (Replacing your more "expensive" employees with cheap young talent could end up costing more than enhancing the workplace experience for experienced players.)

- *The higher you climb the corporate ladder, the more the power trigger becomes important.* There's a clear and steady increase in the desire to be perceived as powerful (starting at entry level to C level). People who make over $50,000 a year are twice as likely to be fascinated by power than those who make under $50,000; if you're trying to fascinate a senior manager, reread the section about the power trigger.

- *Lower-level employees are more fascinated by attractiveness than by power.* (Among this group, appearance is more important than influence.)

- *Only 9 percent say their bosses are "extremely fascinating."* The majority of people don't find their bosses even mildly fascinating. Management training to help leaders engage and inspire might help workplace morale.

- *A few generational differences:* Generations are fascinated differently by work, and by personal life. It's important not only to evaluate which trigger to use with your groups, but, to persuade and influence behavior, you must also customize for their age and professional level. Our priorities change throughout our careers. For instance, eighteen- to twenty-nine-year-olds think having a fascinating career is more important than a fascinating personal life. Looking at the older set, there's a different story. C-level employees say they're more fascinated with their spouses than any other group.

- *Good news if you're hiring*: People would rather be fascinating on a job interview than a first date.

- *Good news if you're firing*: Unemployed people think their lives are more fascinating than those who are employed.

The Role of Fascination in Personal Decision Making

- *If you're considering having a baby* . . . Parents think their lives are far more fascinating than nonparents. Four in five parents become "completely engrossed" in an activity or conversation with their children at least a few times a week, and 63 percent of moms experience this on a daily basis.

- *If you're trying to decide between sending an e-mail or speaking in person* . . . People find in-person conversations four times more fascinating than ones online.

- *If you're thinking about texting someone* . . . It depends on the person's age. Baby boomers aren't very fascinated by their mobile devices, but for younger people their cell phones are "completely engrossing."*

- *If you're thinking about dishing the dirt on divorce . . .*
  82 percent say they're more fascinated by what keeps couples *together* than what breaks them *apart*. Could be the state of the country with such a high divorce rate, but there may be an opportunity for a brand or TV show to celebrate healthy relationships.

- *If you're considering cosmetic surgery . . .*
  People rated "reading books and newspapers" as making someone more fascinating than cosmetic surgery. In addition, people would rather have a conversation with someone who's trustworthy than someone who is attractive.

- *If you're considering stretching the truth . . .*
  64 percent of people are more interested in fact than fiction. (Embellishment also breaks our most important trigger, trust. Find interesting ways to present the truth.)

- *If you want to tempt people to break their rules . . .*
  60 percent say they'd be willing to bend morals and standards to live a more fascinating life. For unmarried people, it goes up to 68 percent. For the majority, it might seem, doing what's "wrong" isn't so wrong if it nets a positive outcome.† Midlevel managers, for instance, are less

---

* This group ranks their cell phones as more fascinating than their own lives!

† Despite the importance of trust, the majority of us are willing to bend our morals in pursuit of a more fascinating life.

worried about telling the truth than other professional segments. People value fascination, and if they have to bend a few morals to do it . . . well, so be it. (For more on the subject, refer to the vice trigger.)

- *If you're thinking about breaking someone's trust* . . . People rate trust in their personal relationships as more important than all the other triggers combined.

- *If you're nervous about taking a risk in your life* . . . Spectacular success is more important than spectacular failure. Risks may be less risky than you think. A big success is a much bigger deal than a failure. When trying to impress the CEO, the news is even better: In this group, 93 percent find spectacular success to be fascinating.

Conclusions

A few final notes of the study:

- *We're bored.* We're overwhelmed by messages, but unsatisfied by the ones we do have. We're doing too much, but are not fascinated by the things we are doing. All those messages and experiences aren't getting the job done. Only 40 percent of us found our lives fascinating in the past year.

- *Most people don't feel fascinating.* We feel shy about admitting that we want to be fascinating, but we do. On a personal level, we want to attract the respect and attention of others. We go to great effort and expense for products and experiences that can help us become more fascinating in the eyes of others.

- *Fascination makes us feel more alive.* In the presence of someone or something that fascinates us, we talk more, react more, and connect more.

- *The three main things we seek: relationships, trust, and fascination.* Relationships, especially with family, fascinate us. Having close bonds raises the quality of our lives and makes us feel more engaged in general. We feel "intensely fascinated" while spending time with the people we love more often than while doing anything else. Trust is the most important trigger, and the one by which we judge ourselves and others in a relationship.

Despite the billions of dollars spent by record companies, fashion designers, and movie directors, what we find most fascinating is spending time with our children and significant others.

On the very first page of the survey, at the top of the page, participants read the following opening statement:

> *For the purpose of this survey, we are describing fascination as an intense captivation. When something is fascinating, it captures your attention in an unusually intense way. It's more than "interesting." It distracts you from other things around you, and makes you want to pay complete attention. You might be fascinated by a favorite book, a project at work, or even a new love. Note that when something is fascinating, it is not inherently good or bad, only that it captures your full attention.*

By the end of the research, it became apparent that in terms of the role fascination plays in our lives, it's more than described above. The respondents told us that fascination is a fundamental part of our relationships and our quality of life. It affects how hard we work, who we marry, even how we feel about ourselves.

Author's Note

Like all things fascinating, the triggers and exercises in this book are not ironclad black and white. Fascination is a constant work in progress, ever changing alongside technology, the environment, consumer attitudes—and your feedback. We're interested to hear about your own triggers, and the results of your exercises from Part III. We're also constantly on the lookout for fresh examples of the ways in which people and companies use triggers. Is your brand fascinating in a particularly remarkable way? Do tell. We're quite keen to hear more.

Fascinate@SallyHogshead.com

We frequently share new findings and observations of how fascination lives in culture, marketing, and everyday life, and you'll find these at SallyHogshead.com. To join our conversation, please feel free to friend and follow:

Facebook.com/Hogshead

Twitter.com/SallyHogshead

Linkedin.com/in/hogshead

In the meantime, thank you for joining this conversation. May all your days be fascinating.

Fascination at a Glance

Overall Principles:
- You are already fascinating, using your natural strengths.
- Anyone, and anything, can become *more* fascinating.
- There are seven fascination triggers, each with a different purpose.
- Fascination is instinctive, innate, and often involuntary.
- Fascination affects every part of our lives.
- Fascination is the shortcut to persuasion.
- Now more than ever, fascination is a new competitive advantage.

Trends Driving the Need for Fascination:
- An overload of distracting choices
- The rise of the ADD world
- Earning attention, not paying attention
- The ability to shut out messages
- Shift from the information age to the fascination age
- The Fascination Economy

Gold Hallmarks of a Fascinating Message:

- Provokes strong and immediate emotional reactions
- Creates advocates
- Becomes "cultural shorthand" for a specific set of actions or values
- Incites conversation
- Forces competitors to realign around it
- Triggers social revolutions

The Seven Triggers

These seven universal triggers spark a variety of responses, any one of which heightens our physical, emotional, and intellectual focus. Effectively activated, each trigger creates a different type of response.

Lust

If you trigger *lust*, you will draw others closer. They will crave your message, wanting more and more until satiated.

Pillars of Lust:

- Stop thinking, start feeling
- Make the ordinary more emotional
- Use all five senses
- Tease and flirt

Mystique

Trigger *mystique*, and you'll encourage others to learn more about your message. They'll be intrigued, and seek information.

Pillars of Mystique:
- Spark curiosity
- Withhold information
- Build mythology
- Limit access

Alarm

With *alarm*, you compel others to behave more urgently. They'll take action in order to avoid negative consequences.

Pillars of Alarm:
- Define consequences
- Create deadlines
- Increase perceived danger
- Focus not on the crisis most *likely*, but on the one most *feared*
- Use distress to steer positive action

Prestige

A message with *prestige* will elevate you above others, inspiring covetousness or envy.

Pillars of Prestige:
- Develop emblems
- Set a new standard
- Limit availability
- Earn it

Power

If you effectively trigger *power*, you will control others. They will defer to you and your message.

Pillars of Power:
- Dominate
- Control the environment
- Reward and punish

Vice

By triggering *vice*, your message will tempt others to deviate from their usual code of conduct. They'll act outside of standard habits or norms.

Pillars of Vice:
- Create taboos
- Lead others astray
- Define absolutes
- Give a wink

Trust

With *trust*, your message will comfort others, relax them, and bind them more closely to you.

Pillars of Trust:
- Become familiar
- Repeat and retell
- Be authentic
- Accelerate trust

Your Potential Fascination Badges

Seven potential areas for what you represent:

Purpose: Your reason for being; your function as a brand.

Core beliefs: The code of values and principles that guides you; what you stand for.

Heritage: Your reputation and history; the "backstory" of how you came to be.

Products: The goods, services, or information you produce.

Benefits: The promises of reward for purchasing the product, both tangible and abstract, overt and implied.

Actions: How you conduct yourself.

Culture: All characteristics of your identity, including personality, executional style, and mind-set.

Steps to Find the Edge of Your Bell Curve:
- List your badges (both existing and potential).
- Evaluate against the hallmarks of a fascinating brand.
- Plot on a bell curve.
- Push badges outward on the curve by infusing them with more of your primary trigger.
- Push badges outward on the curve by infusing them with a new trigger.
- Build your message around these badges.

Who Invented the Seven Triggers?
These seven triggers aren't anything new. I didn't invent them. In fact, you're already using them. You've been using them your whole life.

That very first time you gave your mother a big, toothless smile? You were fascinating then, and you're fascinating now. Every time you make eye contact, you're fascinating. When you teach your kindergartener how to use scissors, or train the dog to stay off the couch, you're fascinating. When you keep a secret, or stand your ground, or fulfill a promise, or hold someone close, you're fascinating because you're using your natural strengths to connect with others.

How will you apply the seven triggers to your own message so that the people around you don't just hear what you're saying, but act upon it? How could you apply this not only to your product and work relationships but to the people and pursuits closest to you? That's the bigger purpose.

Sources

Lust

MARILYN MONROE'S "WET" VOICE: David Huron is professor of music at Ohio State University, and author of *Sweet Anticipation: Music and the Psychology of Expectation* (Cambridge, Mass.: MIT Press, 2008). Over the course of two entirely engrossing interviews, Huron described the effects of a "wet" or "dry" voice, and directed me to John Ohala's work on why humans smile. Huron also described other lust cues not included in this book: Why a certain song can have the power to make us weep (we attach great personal meaning to it), why horror movie sound tracks give us goose bumps (frisson sounds create a state of fear in the spine and lower brain), and why we experience pleasure in those horror movies (endorphine release mimics cocaine and heroin in brain chemicals). Why Cinderella's stepsisters have big feet (foot size is a secondary sex characteristic, so bigger feet make them more masculine). And why Betty Boop is perversely sexual (she's a cutesy voice in a Jessica Rabbit body).

The initial descriptions of Marilyn Monroe's voice come from a 2006 NPR program, when commentator Brian McConnachie played her voice, and asked his listeners to describe it.

Mystique

JÄGERMEISTER: Seth Stevenson's May 21, 2005, *New York* magazine article, "The Cocktail Creationist," is chock-full of juicy marketing stories about liquor baron Sidney Frank. (For more information, see also Grey Goose in the prestige trigger.) With stories on Jägermeister, Corazón, and Grey Goose, this article also might offer prospects for your next night out.

Championship poker: Jeff "Happy" Shulman shared many terrific insider secrets about the world of high-stakes poker. Shulman, editor of *Card Player* magazine, also gave us the phrase, "Information is the opposite of mystique."

Alarm

DRUNK DRIVING AND THE PROM DATE: To confirm details on this example, I interviewed Luke Sullivan in 2009. However, it dates back a bit further. Sullivan was my mentor at my first job at Fallon McElligott advertising agency in Minneapolis, in 1993, and this particular ad was formative in my career.

JAY GNOSPELIUS: To write the case study on Jay Gnospelius, I spent several weeks interviewing and researching Jay's history, and the topics of suicide and amputation as they relate to the alarm trigger. I grasped the topic more fully while Jay and I were eating dinner together one night in New York. Jay ordered the steak, very rare, then said to the waiter, "Could you please ask the chef to cut the meat into small bites?" I didn't understand why . . . at first.

Prestige

TULIP HYSTERIA: The history of the tulip economic bubble has been well documented by economists, botanists, and historians. The first known example is the 1637 hand-illustrated manuscript *The Tulip Book of P. Cos.* Charles Mackay described the bubble in his 1848 book, *Memoirs of Extraordinary Popular Delusions and the Madness of Crowds* (Boston: L. C. Page and Company, 1932). More recently, Peter M. Garber wrote about it in "Famous First Bubbles," for the *Journal of Economic Perspectives* 4, 2 (Spring 1990): 35–54.

Power

DOMINIQUE MOCEANU: In 2008, Dominique Moceanu spoke out against the Karolyis, and the physical and mental toll female gymnasts face. The debate appears in many publications, including a *New York Times* article on July 22, 2008, by Juliet Macur, titled, "Amid Harsh Words for the Karolyis from Ex-Gymnasts, a Question: How Much Is Too Much?" (This is not the first time Moceanu earned the public's fascination for controversy. In 1999, Frank Litsky of the *New York Times* reported on the "bitter dispute" between Dominique Moceanu and her father, Dumitru, which included a clash over $1 million in earnings, a restraining order that kept him at least 500 feet away from his daughter, and perhaps most notably, accusations that Dumitru was trying to kill two of Moceanu's friends.)

LANDMARK EDUCATION: For the extensive research involved in this case study, we've tried to present an even-handed snapshot that allows us to draw upon Landmark's techniques, while still exploring the organization's uncommonly intense

use of the power trigger. Maintaining objectivity isn't as easy
as it might sound. Research about Landmark is plentiful and
varied, but also controversial and biased (both *for* and *against*
the organization). Landmark has many vocal detractors,
such as cult expert Rick Ross. A *Washington Post* 1992 story
by Robert F. Howe was titled "Self-Help Course Allegedly
Shattered a Life." Al Lock, corporate training consultant,
attended the Forum course, and describes the "brainwashing
process" in a November 6, 2008, *Bangkok Post* article, "Train
the Trainer: The Landmark Debate."

Landmark Education itself offers a great deal of constructive, objective research on its own site at LandmarkEducation
.com, including the quoted studies by Yankelovich and IMC,
Inc. This case study also draws upon my own personal (positive)
experience in Landmark courses in the early 1990s.

Vice

DARE: There's a great deal of documentation in the media
about DARE's lack of success. For example, the United States
Government Accounting (now Accountability) Office (GAO)
report issued in 2006 provided no evidence that the program
was effective in reducing alcohol or drug abuse, which was
earlier identified as the "central question to be addressed by
the study." Our research for this case study included working
closely with Dr. Linn Goldberg, professor of medicine at the
Oregon Health and Science University, head of the Division of
Health Promotion and Sports Medicine, and co-developer of
the drug-prevention and health-promotion programs ATLAS
and ATHENA, sponsored by the National Institute on Drug
Abuse (NIDA). Additional phone interviews included Rocky
Anderson, former mayor of Salt Lake City (and outspoken

critic of DARE), and Dr. Kelli Komro, who developed Project
Northland (called "DARE Plus"), a successful alcohol-
prevention program, while at the University of Minnesota.

There are a number of programs that do actually work and
are endorsed by the National Institute of Drug Abuse. Examples include Atlas/Athena, Life Skills Training, Project Alert,
and Project Northland. Each has unique attributes and is right
for different age groups and targets, but all produce effective,
positive results for preventing drug use.

Trust

EDIBLE SCHOOLYARD: We worked with Carolyn Federman,
director of development at Chez Panisse Foundation, to learn
about the program's premise and day-to-day application.
Alice Waters's lovely book *Edible Schoolyard: A Universal Idea*
(San Francisco: Chronicle Books, 2008) offers descriptions
of the program, photographs of the gardens, and first-person
accounts from students. Waters writes, "Right there, in the
middle of every school day, lie time and energy already de-
voted to feeding the children. We have the power to turn that
school lunch from an afterthought into a joyous education,
a way of caring for our health, our environment, and our
community."

Huge thanks to my principal investigator, Gabe Goldberg, for
his research skills, insight, and creative collaboration throughout the project. Mr. Goldberg is a marketing executive living
in New York City who has worked with some of the biggest
brands and most respected companies in the world, including
JWT (formerly J. Walter Thompson), Unilever, Condé Nast,
Time, Inc., and Starbucks Coffee Company.

Acknowledgments

Thank you to my spectacular agents, Larry Kirshbaum and Jud Laghi; my brilliant editor, Ben Loehnen; the assistant editor, Matthew Inman; the team at HarperCollins; Linda Jeo Zerba and Deputy Consulting; Sabrina Ross Lee; and my speaking coaches, Nick Morgan and Nikki Smith-Morgan. And thank you to my beloved assistant and friend, Cynthia Gaskin.

So many people on Facebook and Twitter contributed ideas that in a sense this book is a collaboration with all of them. Thank you for making this book more fascinating! For a complete list, please see www.SallyHogshead.com/thanks.

Finally and most of all, to my incredible family, I thank you with all my heart.

Index